Praise for Angel Hero

"An enchanting narrative examining how love transcends all, especially our three-dimensional, physical world. Angel Hero will inspire you to have faith in the universe."

—Rob Bignell, Author,
Windmill and Love Letters to Sophie's Mom

"Angel Hero is alive with feeling, both sexual and spiritual. By turns vivid and gritty, ethereal and romantic, this exquisite book tells a love story that evokes laughter, tears, and wonder in equal measure."

—Elaine Leilani Madison, Ph.D.,
Professor of Literature, emerita, Hawai'i Pacific University

"Lizbeth Hartz has a knack for choosing just the right word to paint the most compelling picture possible. From the moment I began reading Angel Hero, I was totally engaged. The interplay of refreshing humor and spine-tingling suspense had me alternately laughing and grabbing the edge of my chair. Part romance, part crime, part spiritual, and all heart, Angel Hero will take you on a wild ride you won't ever forget."

—Pratibha S. Eastwood Ph.D., STA/ISST, S.E.P., Author

"Perhaps we should propose a new category of memoir, a 'true crime, true love' genre, because that's precisely where *Angel Hero,* Lizbeth Hart's otherworldly, romance-murder mystery would fit. *Angel Hero* is an engrossing and rewarding read. It is not to be missed."

—Alice Folkart, novelist, memoirist, widely-published poet

ANGEL HERO

Murder in Hawai'i – A True Story

LIZBETH HARTZ

Angel Hero Murder in Hawai'i - A True Story
Copyright © Lizbeth Hartz 2014
ISBN: 978-84-946149-0-3
First printing April 2014
Third Edition October 2016 Kwill Books
www.kwillbooks.com

All rights reserved. Except for brief passages quoted in newspaper, magazine, radio, television, or online reviews, no portion of this book may be reproduced, distributed, or transmitted in any form by any means, electronic or mechanical, including photocopying, recording, or information storage or retrieval system, without the prior written permission of the author.

For almighty God and that stylin' dude Vic

Author's Note

A FREELANCE WRITER since 1983, I credit my daily writing routine with enabling me to fulfill the vow I made to Vic in 1985. "I'll keep honing my writing skills," I promised, "until I can craft such a compelling story people will clamor to read it."

I also vowed to tell the truth about the inspirational spiritual events that occurred. I have kept that promise.

However, for three decades, I disguised what took place in the physical world of time and space as fiction. I wrote a dozen different versions of this story, most of them novels. The last thing I wanted was for the gunman to find out what I'd written about him.

In October 2015, the second edition of *Angel Hero* was published. I continued camouflaging people's identities, altering their names and appearances, and changing dates and locations. When my memories of actual words spoken faded, I scripted conversations so as to evoke the feeling and meaning of what was said.

Because I fictionalized only the names, dates, locations and appearances, I called the book a fictionalized memoir. To be precise, a true crime, true love fictionalized memoir.

In this third edition of *Angel Hero*, the Who, When, and Where as described above remain altered. The story itself remains true. My new publisher, Kwill Books, assigned additional non-fiction romance and crime genres to the book. *Angel Hero* takes place on Oahu in the early Eighties.

Prologue

Autumn 1973

In October, I took a palmistry class from a kind-faced grandmother wearing a purple muumuu who advertised herself as "Aurora the Clairvoyant Palmist." A few days later, I signed up for a reading.

Smoke from sandalwood-scented candles wafted over me as I faced her across a round table in her tapestry-hung room. The moment the white-haired, green-eyed woman touched my hand, my heart pounded so hard it hurt. I sobbed convulsively. *Oh my god. I'm having a nervous breakdown.*

"Ah, I see you're sensitive, Goldilocks. It's just past-life sorrow, dear." Aurora offered me a tissue and ran a purple fingernail lightly across my palm. "See the cross connecting your lifeline and your heart line? That's a psychic cross."

I blew my nose. "My mother called me her little witch Lizzy."

"Well, Liz, you could develop your psychic ability further if you continued learning palmistry, and practiced reading palms." She studied my right hand. "Was your father present when you were growing up?"

"When he wasn't flying B-52s for the Air Force."

Aurora pointed to a depression below where my second finger met my palm. "See this? The lack of a mound tells me you lacked a male role model growing up."

I started crying again. I just couldn't help it. "Dad was hardworking and honest, but I never knew when his pressure-cooker career would cause him to explode in anger. As a child, I both loved and feared him."

She said softly, "You still carry heartbreak in your aura from longing for, but lacking, a man's love." She told me I'd carried the heartache into this life from a prior lifetime.

"You loved a married man. He asked you to become his mistress, as was the custom of the times." The woman said the idea of unsanctified sex had scared me so badly I withdrew to the Church, where I made spiritual gains through prayer and meditation. "Hence your psychic ability now. But you hurt yourself retreating like that. Such withdrawal is a kind of suicide. God wants you to say yes to life, not run from it."

She told me that, if I could break out of my shell and learn to speak up for myself, I might experience an exalted spiritual relationship with a man in this lifetime and beyond.

"But be careful not to fall for emotionally distant, angry men like your dad," she cautioned, "lest you perpetuate the heartache that has plagued you so long."

Chapter 1

August 1981, Eight Years Later

MINUTES BEFORE MIDNIGHT, in an unlit parking lot on Fort Craig, a sudden rain saran-wrapped my red muumuu to my tall, slim frame. Shivering, I sprinted through the velvet night past tall palm trees, their fronds clattering in the brisk trade winds, to an old concrete building. The front door creaked open, and I hurried down a dark hallway to a cold room where I dispatched fire trucks for the Army.

I shivered harder. A friend, Fire Captain Keoki, offered me his warm jacket and kissed my cheek, Hawai'ian style. He'd stopped by after a late alarm to tell me about a rare vacancy for an experienced dispatcher at Whaler Air Force Base in central Oahu.

"They've got a high-tech office, Liz. Not like here." He pointed at the fire alarm system where alarms clacked in by punch tape, *rat tat, rat, tat,* three times when the decrepit old thing worked the way it should. "The Whaler chief's big on education, not like Skinny Ski. And you'd get to work solo."

I wrapped Keoki's jacket tightly around me. "Thanks. You're a pal." I pointed at my dispatching partner, a sixty-something World War Two vet. Oblivious to Keoki and me, he puffed on a cigar and stared at a blaring TV show. "Work solo, yes!" I said softly.

The next day, I applied for the federal civil service dispatching job at Whaler. I hoped to land the job based on my reputation as a capable dispatcher and the excellent performance ratings my supervisor, Pete Polawski, had given me before the last, bad one.

Pete and I had been on friendly terms until the previous May, when he announced refresher training would start on the following day shift. He told me I wouldn't be working my night shift schedule for the next two weeks.

"I signed a contract to teach English on my mornings off starting next week," I said. "Can you please postpone the refresher training?"

Pete refused, saying he'd already made up the schedule.

How difficult is it to grab a pen and change it? Why didn't you give me some notice? I thought, but did not say.

"This job comes first," he added.

The old familiar acidy feeling in my stomach and churning in my gut accompanied Pete's inflexible refusal. Anxiety around authority figures made speaking up harder for me than pulling hen's teeth. I figured that pleading my case to Pete wouldn't do any good anyway, and went over his head. The training officer gave me the okay to teach now and train later.

Pete must have gone berserk on the guy because, the next day, the training officer told me he'd been mistaken. His voice shaking, he said he didn't have the authority to postpone my training after all. I cursed Pete under my breath and cancelled my teaching contract. Pete punished my audacity with a poor rating, the first step toward being fired.

* * *

A month later, after I applied for the dispatcher job with the Air Force, at four o'clock shift change, Pete tersely briefed me on alarms in progress. I nodded, my gut cramping at the hostility in his voice. He grabbed his briefcase and stomped away, his yellow raincoat ballooning around his stick-thin body, the metal exit door clanging shut behind him.

"Jerk," I muttered. I was still waiting and hoping. I thought I'd come across pretty well in a phone interview the week before with Chief Green at Whaler Fire Department, but he'd given me no indication he might select me as his new dispatcher.

Rodney, my dispatching partner, chuckled. "Ah, never mind Skinny

Ski. He's probably being a piss ant because his wife ain't giving him any."

I smiled. "You're a pal to try and cheer me up."

A phone jangled on the dusty alarm panel. Keeping one eye on a spider swinging on a silk strand from the cobweb-laced ceiling, I hurried to the console. Maybe I'd get lucky and find a better job before Pete gave me another unsatisfactory rating. Story of my life, wanting to escape from the devil I knew, hoping the devil I didn't would be better.

I pushed the phone switch forward. "Fire Department, Liz speaking."

"Hello, Liz."

Recognizing the voice, I inhaled sharply. "Hello, Chief Green."

"I'll get right to the point," he said. "My sources say your poor rating from Pete is undeserved. Would you like to work for me?"

"Oh yes, sir."

"You're hired."

"Thank you, chief! You won't regret it."

I beamed at Rodney. He laughed. "Somebody's grinning like the Cheshire cat. Did you just get hired for the only federal dispatching job open on Oahu?"

I sprang from my chair, throwing my arms in the air. "Yes siree!"

He hugged me and said he would miss me but was glad I could quit worrying about Pete getting me fired. I hugged him back, happy my eighteen-month dispatching career would continue, and I could still be a link in the emergency response chain when crises came down fast and hot.

Two weeks later, I said goodbye to my friends, good riddance to Pete, and sayonara to Fort Craig. The following Monday, I walked through the freshly painted, Air Force-blue door of Whaler's centralized fire station. I looked forward to working solo in a clean, high tech office, hopefully with a less rigid boss.

* * *

Except for my two closest girlfriends, Carey and Julie, no one knew about the emotional baggage I carried with me when I transferred from Fort Craig to Whaler. Baggage made heavy by two previous boyfriends, both of whom had dumped me for other women.

After the second one hit the dusty trail, I told myself, *if there's a next time, it has to be with a faithful guy.* I spun romantic scenarios about a courtship with a man who communicated well and would want to commit before sex muddied the waters. Mr. Right would be someone who wouldn't criticize, embarrass, or fail to love me; someone as different from my philandering lovers as Bambi was from Bluebeard. *Someday My Prince Will Come* became my theme song.

I met intelligent, courteous, part-Hawai'ian Billy in a Hawai'ian history course at the college where I taught yoga. Despite me being a haole, local slang for Caucasian, whose ancestors had stolen his people's land and culture, we hit it off. Several months of intense conversations over cafeteria lunches convinced me I had found what I sought in him.

However, after we moved in together, the hang-ups we'd kept hidden—the anger exploding out of him at haoles, my fear of abandonment and speaking up—plagued our relationship. But there was far more joy than pain for the first five years. The GI bill paid for his schooling and the Army hired me as a clerk, so we didn't worry about money. We hiked, swam, and studied Hawai'ian history together. I helped him edit his assignments. He was caring and faithful. We seemed to be bridging the cultural gap between us.

By the time I transferred to Whaler Fire Department, the bridge had weakened. Billy graduated, his money stopped, and his anger ignited more frequently. I worried when we talked less and argued more. My feelings for him still ran deep, but I longed for a sunnier partner, someone I could talk to who would really hear me.

September 1981, at Whaler

Irene Choshu's bouffant hairdo was an echo from the Fifties, when she'd been a teenager. Her bright red nails, violent exclamation points against her hands, perfectly matched the oval lips in her pretty round face. As the senior day-shift alarm room dispatcher at Whaler, she doubled as my trainer. When the chief introduced us, she smiled and said, "We're glad you're here, Liz. Just ask the firemen pulling your shifts. They'll tell you."

She kept the alarm room stinking of cigarette smoke and as cold as a north wind. During my two weeks of training on day shift, she thoughtfully excused herself when she needed a smoke. As soon as a qualified alarm room operator sat in for her, her high heels clicked quickly across the open bay garage until she lit up beside a smelly trash can where the smokers hung out.

Under Irene's excellent tutorship, I learned how to operate the high-tech radios and digital alarm panel, dispatch structural trucks to buildings, airfield trucks to airplanes, and emergency repairmen to base housing. She taught me how to perform alarm notifications, type up reports, and compile stats for the chief. When one of the forty-some firefighters on A- and B-shifts stopped by to meet me, Irene introduced us.

During my first week at Whaler, as I sat rubbing the backs of my chilled hands against my jeans, two firemen strolled into the alarm room. One of them, a tall man with tanned smile lines around his eyes and a Mr. Universe physique, leaned against the doorway. The other, a short, round man with bushy eyebrows and a thick mat of tightly coiled black hair, stood with legs spread and hands on his hips.

Irene nodded at the shorter man. "Liz, this is Jaku Cardoza. He operates the turret on the P-15, that big yellow truck at the end of the stalls." Nodding at the weight lifter and pointing at a red truck through the picture window, she added, "And this is Vic Lazzarini, solo driver of Ramp 7, that rapid-response pickup parked next to the chief's. Jaku and Vic, Lizbeth Hartz."

"Please call me Liz," I said.

Jaku's undershirt, visible where his buttoned blue uniform shirt gaped open across the widest part of his belly, looked like a misplaced, white eye. His grin was wide and warm. "Welcome, Liz." He raised his bushy eyebrows up and down, Groucho Marx style. I smiled. He added, "Take a smoke break, Irene?"

"Liz isn't qualified yet," she said.

"We'll cover for you," Jaku offered.

She hesitated, looked at me. "Okay with you, Liz?"

"Sure."

She thanked Jaku, picked up her cigarette pack and lighter, and hurried outside.

The moment she disappeared, Jaku grabbed my cold hand in his warm one and looked me over from my blue tennis shoes to my blonde curls. "The guys say you're one fine *wahine*." He repeated his Groucho Marx routine. I wondered if a knife had caused the scar zigzagging across his forehead. "The buggers no lie."

"Thank you." I retracted my hand.

The other man, Vic, raised an eyebrow at Jaku and shoved his large hands in his pockets. "Nice to meet you," he said, his voice low and deep.

"Likewise." I noticed the dimples in his cheeks and his deep blue eyes.

The red airfield emergency phone rang. I grabbed the phone and started scribbling runway and tail numbers. Vic and Jaku sprinted to their trucks, and Irene ran back to the alarm room. I pushed a red button to send one wailing tone through the station, and repeated my broadcast twice over the radio, "Inflight emergency, hot brakes, C-5 tail number 147, landing Runway Six Right in two minutes."

Through the picture window, I saw firemen pulling the straps of heat-resistant, silver turn-out overalls over their shoulders as they ran. Vic's Ramp 7 pickup truck screech-wheeled out of the station, leading the way. The enormous airfield trucks revved their engines loudly before following, looking like lumbering elephants pursuing a speedy jaguar.

"Why do the brakes get hot before the plane even lands?" I asked Irene.

"Sometimes the hydraulics controlling the mechanisms that slow the plane down don't work right." She helped me make the required notifications, and showed me how to fill out the log sheet and punch the vehicle run cards.

"Bachelor buddies, those two," she told me. "Jaku's a character. Vic's a loner."

On the following shift, I dispatched my first non-airfield alarm, an unattended cooking fire in base housing, sending three loud wailing tones through the station. Seconds later, I announced an engine start standby for an F-4 fighter plane and watched through the large picture window as Ramp 7 burned rubber out of the airfield truck stalls.

When A-shift returned to duty the next day, Jaku sauntered into the alarm room, nodded at Irene, grinned at me, and said, "The B-shift guys say you're one hot haole on the radio."

I smiled politely, even though I disliked being called a haole, which literally meant devoid of breath, meaning spirit. Since Billy had clued me in that islanders considered the term synonymous with Caucasian and not derogatory unless they added "f . . . ing" in front of it, I did not take offense.

"Take a smoke break, Irene?" he asked.

The moment Irene walked out the door, Jaku dove into tales about his Navy days. He gestured and strutted, his whole body punctuating stories about his bravado and the wild haole nurses he'd known, and I was haole, too, wasn't I?

"Haole, yes, wild, no," I said. "I've lived with my boyfriend for five years."

"That dark-skinned local dude drove you here yesterday?"

I nodded.

"You're all right, Liz." He wiggled his eyebrows at me. "You're cool. You ain't the kind of stuck-up haole broad who thinks you ain't right if you ain't white." I opened my mouth to say thanks but he sped on with, "Bet you never knew I was stationed on an aircraft carrier in 'Nam'."

I shook my head.

He plunged into a pantomime, demonstrating how he fought fires caused by bombs falling with a "kaboom!" He slammed his body against the alarm room's stained brown carpet, sprang up, dragged an imaginary fire hose, and extinguished the flames "that were all around" accompanied by the "whoosh, whoosh" of water from his hose.

His performance was funny and animated. I laughed and he worked his invisible hose harder. Irene was right. This guy was a character.

A few days later, when the fire engines roared back into the station after I dispatched an alarm in the barracks, Vic and Jaku walked into the alarm room. We were making small talk when Jaku wriggled his eyebrows and pulled three Polaroid snapshots from his pocket. He held them up, saying, "See these pictures me and Lazzarini took of each other?"

The pictures showed Vic and Jaku at the wash rack beside the Ramp pickup, bare-chested and soaked, their right hands shoved down the front of their shorts, Jaku leering, a silly grin on Vic's face.

Irene raised her eyebrows. "Oh, Vic," she said.

Vic turned to Jaku. "Aww, why'd you show them those? Now they'll think I'm a . . . a pervert."

Jaku nodded and grinned. "I thought that's what we were, brah."

Uneasiness pricked me like pins, that Jaku would embarrass his friend so readily, seemingly just to grab the spotlight of Irene's and my attention. What kind of friendship allowed for this? Why did they strike those pathetic poses to begin with?

Busy as I was learning the facets of my new dispatching job and meeting the firefighters and inspectors and secretaries and extinguisher shop guys, I didn't think about the two mismatched friends until I saw Vic on the following Wednesday night.

I had graduated to working the night shift solo. When the swing shift dispatcher left at midnight, I locked the door and changed the 24-hour reel-to-reel recording tapes.

When I wasn't reading, typing reports, or writing in the log books, I dimmed the overhead lights so I wouldn't be visible as I kept watch over the airfield trucks through the picture window's one-way glass, and over the parking lot through the tiny back window. Except for swaying palm fronds and a black cat streaking through the parking lot, the only movement I saw that night was a fireman hurrying from his bunk to the bathroom. He ducked down when he passed the alarm room's picture window so I wouldn't see him and ask for a bathroom break.

The alarm console in the darkened room reminded me of the cockpit of one of the B-52 bombers my Air Force pilot father flew. The small red, yellow and green lights illuminated the black surfaces of the instrument panels sitting atop the L-shaped console. Red digital numbers glowed from the clock above the slowly turning magnetic tapes in the back. The radio alarm screen letters shone luminescent green. A red scan light ran continuously across ten radio channels, pausing only when someone spoke.

The red airfield phone rang at 2 a.m. I turned up the lights and copied the tower operator's message: an in-flight emergency on a C-5 cargo plane that had lost its number two engine and would try to land on runway Four Right.

God help us. My voice shook as I dispatched the alarm and visualized the plane flying lopsided, unable to land with a hole where the engine had been.

The assistant chief, Master Sergeant Maxwell—the guys called him Mad Max because he was so tense and angry—radioed in, "Control, did the engine actually fall off?"

"Ye . . . ye . . . yes," I stuttered. "They . . . didn't say 'number two engine shutdown,' like they usually do. They said the . . . the engine was lost."

A few minutes later, Max announced, "Emergency terminated, Control. By the way, the engine is still securely fastened to the plane." He chuckled.

"Ten-four," I whispered. My face heated up. *They'll think I'm green as new grass.*

Vic's pickup was the first to screech back into the station. Still clad in his bulky silver fire retardant overalls, he strode into the alarm room. "We looked all up and down the runway." He shrugged. "No engine anywhere. Where do you suppose it went?"

"Into the ocean?" I wondered if I had turned as red as his Ramp 7 pickup truck.

He laughed loudly and then I did too, until my sides ached.

How rare and reassuring, for a man to approach a mistake of mine with humor rather than criticism or ridicule. Vic's response gave me the confidence to speak up for myself. "I've never heard an engine shutdown called lost engine before. I—"

"Right, right," he interrupted, "the Army doesn't have an airfield, do they?"

I shook my head. "No, so—"

He interrupted again, "So you only dispatched brush fires, and alarms in base housing, right?"

I nodded. "So I didn't know."

"Of course not. How could you?"

"Well . . ." I gave myself a few moments to think about it. "I guess I couldn't."

From that moment on, there wasn't much Vic Lazzarini could do wrong in my eyes.

Three of the returning firemen strode into the alarm room. One of them christened me Dizzy Lizzy. Another asked if I'd heard the blonde joke about the dispatcher who announced, "A little ole engine fell off a big ole plane." The third guy teased me about airfield emergency terminology until Vic growled, "So how's she supposed to know lost number two engine means the same thing as engine shutdown? Ain't you ever made a mistake, Peanut Head?"

The firemen held up their hands, said, "Whoa!" and split.

Grateful that this kind Adonis had stood up for me, I said, "Thank you," and wished I could think of better words.

"That's cool, that's cool." Vic's high-amp grin lit up the room. "I'm gonna mosey on out now." He strode away with a slapstick saunter, looking especially humorous in his bulky overalls.

I later christened that strut of his "Stylin' Dude Walk."

During my next two weeks at Whaler, I didn't see Vic much. At first, he didn't pop into the alarm room to "talk story," local slang for shooting the breeze. But always, unlike most of the firemen, Vic offered me a bathroom break whenever he woke up in the night. I never turned him down, hoping to avoid needing another break during my shift while everyone slept. Without a bathroom in the alarm room, I had to summon the relief fireman via the public address system piped into the bunkroom. His three bunkmates usually woke up, too, all of them angry.

I hated waking four men just to pee. So I talked to Clyde, a fireman whose morning cleanup duties included emptying the trash, about the feasibility of turning the lights down low and relieving myself in disposable coffee cups with lids.

"Brilliant idea," he said. "With the lights low, no one can see you through the one-way glass. For insurance, you can hide in that supply closet." He pointed to two skinny doors at the back of the room.

Because I didn't want anyone to know what I was doing, I buried all the filled cups in the bottom of the trashcan's black plastic bag rather than carry them to a toilet. Some of the guys noticed I wasn't waking them up as often. When they said they appreciated my thoughtfulness in drinking less liquid on night shifts, I simply smiled.

I was starting to feel more comfortable in my job when an Army friend, Assistant Fire Chief Ron Lee, secured an emergency nearby after midnight. He drove to the Whaler station to talk with me. I had dimmed the lights to toss a cup of pee in the trash when I spotted him walking toward the alarm room.

Ron said the guys missed my clear voice on the radio and assured me that everyone, with the possible exception of Skinny Ski, wished me well. He shared some gossip, then left a few minutes later.

I didn't think about his visit until the next day, when three of the paramedic guys strolled into the alarm room and eyed me lasciviously. One of them said, "Ooh, girl! Jaku's talking trash about you and some Army fire dude doing the dirty on the floor last night."

"What?" My heart raced. "Chief Lee dropped by after a . . . a . . . a late alarm," I stammered. "But we weren't . . ." My face and neck burned.

Jaku had told them he was listening to a music tape in his car after midnight when he spotted a red fire chief's pickup truck in front of the station and the alarm room lights dimmed. He said he peered in the back window and saw us having kinky sex on the stained brown carpet.

"I live with my boyfriend, Billy," I stammered, "and I don't . . ."

My distress metamorphosed into anger. "Next time I see Jaku, I'll give that lewd little liar a piece of my mind."

The guys walked out except for Brian Smith, who told me, "We laugh at Jaku's stories but we know, if you wanted to make love, you wouldn't do it on a hard dirty floor." He assured me most of the guys knew that Jaku, whose real name was Christian, was a liar. "So no need to worry."

"Thanks." I relaxed. "I feel better. Next time I see Christian—"

"Don't ever call him Christian," Brian interrupted. "You'd best do nothing."

"Why not?"

"Because Jaku gets even with people in nasty ways if he thinks they're crossing him. Like he tried to do with me after I yelled at him when the lazy bum tried to sneak out of station cleanup." Brian and Jaku had duked it out until Jaku cried uncle. They shook hands afterwards, and Jaku pitched in. "So I thought everything was cool between us."

But the following week, when the two men were hunting pigs in the Koolau Mountains, Brian taking point, Jaku yelled, "Brah, I've got a beef to settle with you."

Brian looked back to see Jaku running toward him with rifle raised. Jaku tripped on a tree root, the gun fired, and the bullet hit Jaku's toe. He screamed like a banshee, blood gushing from his shoe.

"So I bandaged him up," Brian said. "He kept thanking me, but I knew that bullet had my name on it. Now I avoid the locals. You should too, Liz."

Brian didn't know my boyfriend was born and raised in Hawai'i, so I let his comment slide. The locals-versus-mainland haoles conflict was alive and pervasive in the islands. Most of the time, the clash seemed to be one of culture rather than ethnicity. Even so, perhaps because so many different racial groups simmered in the melting pot of Hawai'i, racism was prevalent. After I got to know Vic, one trait I liked in him was that he, like me, seemed to be race and color blind.

"How did he get the nickname Jaku?" I asked.

Brian shook his head. "He adopted it after a Japanese fireman called him 'jaaku no,' meaning 'evil-minded one.' Jaku loved it and wore the name like a badge of glory. "

"Why is a spooky guy like Jaku working here?"

"For one thing, he's a damn good fireman." Brian thought most of the firemen, including Vic, just figured Jaku for a little guy trying to act big. "Relax, Liz. Don't confront him and he won't bother you. He don't bother me no more. I just stay out of his way."

I vowed to never, ever, say or do anything to upset Jaku Cardoza.

A few hours later, I sat at the console, logging some standbys in the pass-on book, when Jaku hurried through the door. He hovered over me, so close I smelled his sour sweat. "I never said you was . . . doing him," he said. "Some asshole's lying to you, trying to make brother Jaku look bad. Who told you that?"

Not wanting to name names, I said, "Lots of people."

He opened his mouth, closed it, paused, shrugged. "All I said was I saw a red fire chief's car parked in front of the station and you two in the alarm room. And who knows? You might've been getting it on. Hey, I wouldn't blame the guy, pretty lady like you. I never mean for upset you."

Liar. "Well . . . if all you said was 'might,' I accept your apology."

"Cool your old man's a local dude like me." He smiled. "You're all right, Liz."

"Thanks," I said, thinking *Billy's nothing like you, asshole.*

Winking, he repeated, "You're all right," and strolled out the door.

* * *

A few days after Jaku's anemic apology, my paramedic pal Tom, a gossipy, intelligent man who kept his jumbo-sized ears pressed to the grapevine, told me Vic thought me being a one-man woman was cool. "Are you really, Liz?"

I nodded and wondered if any woman would answer, "No, I fool around."

"Darn. After what Jaku said about you, we hoped you were a wild woman like Sheila."

I had heard the gossip about Sheila, a young military dispatcher stationed at Whaler a few years prior, and the firemen who stopped by the alarm room for more than conversation when she worked midnight shifts. Sheila got pregnant, the potential sperm donors refused to marry her, and she was booted out of the Air Force, taking her A- or B-shift baby with her.

"Consider your hopes dashed," I said. "Why does Vic like me being faithful to Billy?"

"Because he figures he won't have to deal with you chasing him." Tom shook his balding head. "Vic's shy with women, attracts them like iron filings to a magnet, but runs from all those hotly pursuing bouncing babes, the moron. Dumber than dirt."

"This makes me like him more," I said, charmed that my having a steady gave Vic the green light to relax around me, the naïve new dispatcher who thought engines fell from planes.

A few weeks after Jaku tried to trash my reputation, and the day after another silly fight with Billy, I sat at the alarm room console, despairing about him and me. Gazing through the picture window at golden wisps of clouds scattered across the smoky sky, I escaped into a fantasy about honeymooning in Paris with the tall, darkly handsome Prince Charming I had yet to meet.

The trade winds blew a misty rain, the kind locals called pineapple juice, against the northeast side of the station.

Vic clearing his throat startled me out of my reverie. A smile punched dimples in his cheeks. "Thought I'd mosey on by," he said. "Need a break?"

My first thought, *what's wrong with you, hanging out with Jaku?* dissolved in the memory of him standing up for me. "Yes. Thanks." I wasn't about to say no to this humorous man's thoughtful offer.

When I hurried back from the restroom by the chief's office on the other side of the station, Vic remained seated at the back desk. My heartbeat quickened at the realization he had sought me out to talk.

He amused me with a story about a fireman who, an hour after he was told to polish the engine—engine being a common term for a fire truck—was discovered diligently applying wax to the truck's huge eight-cylinder engine.

After my laughter subsided, I shrugged. "Well, at least he found the engine. My lost engine was never found."

Vic grinned. "You suppose it's laying behind a sand dune *makai*—that's ocean side to you, haole—of Runway Six Right?"

"Nope, I figure it's *mauka*—toward the mountain, Italiano, in case you didn't know."

When I mentioned I taught yoga at a college nearby, Vic christened me, "Miss Yogurt Teachah." Afterwards, when he stopped by the alarm room, he would ask, "Take a break, Snake?" He said he called me Snake because all that yoga made me slither, like I had no bones.

"Sure, GL, thanks," I'd say. GL for greased lightning, the firemen's nickname for this fastest-to-the-fire-scene guy. I would rush to the bathroom and back, hoping we'd have a little time to chat.

I told my good friend and confidante, Julie, about Vic. "I feel like I've found a funny comrade in arms who's so very different from the other testosterone-driven foot soldiers."

Her laughter reminded me of a pig snorting and never failed to propel me into gasping chuckles until my sides ached. I caught my breath, adding, "It's cool he shares my slightly bent sense of humor."

"Slightly?" she screamed, and we cracked up again.

Vic's generosity and droll humor seemed as different from Jaku's lying, attention-hound ways as a bright star is from a black hole. When I worried about Vic having a hidden dark side drawing him to Jaku, my relationship with Billy made me feel safe. Although Billy could be unexpectedly angry, he was faithful and didn't hang out with a deviant friend. I had to admit Vic intrigued me, and started checking the manning sheet to see if he was on duty.

After what Tom had told me, I didn't wring my hands worrying about Vic believing Jaku's lies. But I did worry some. I had witnessed firsthand how quickly lies spread from mouth to mouth through the island's small community of civilian firefighters working for the military.

* * *

Six months earlier, in May 1981, when I was dispatching on Fort Craig, a married fire captain, Glen Cordeiro, repeatedly phoned the dispatch office. His smoker's voice sounded deep and breathy when he asked me to meet him after work at midnight.

"We'll watch the sunrise in each other's arms, gorgeous," he rasped.

I told him, "I've got a boyfriend, and aren't you married?"

"Tell him you're working overtime, pretty. My wife and I are separated."

Back in the early Eighties, sexual harassment wasn't talked about much. Because I wasn't bad to look at, I had attracted my share of propositions, but all from guys who had the grace to accept no for an answer. It alarmed me when Glen kept hounding me.

I hoped he would disappear. He didn't. The stress of a month of his propositions finally gave introverted me the sass to say, "Okay. I'll just phone your . . . separated wife and ask her how you like your eggs."

He quit calling. I relaxed until a fireman who crewed on Glen's truck cued me in that the man was bragging about having hot sex with me in his car after midnight.

I am slow to anger but this news made me burn. Furious, I complained to the Army fire chief, who yelled at Glen and ordered him to apologize to me. Back then, my supervisor, Pete, still approved of me. He laughed when red-faced Glen whispered, "I'm sorry, Liz."

"You should be." I doubted he was, and hoped the Army firemen didn't believe his lies.

Now I wondered if Jaku had heard the rumor, and if it played into his lies about me. I hoped, if the Whaler firemen had heard Glen's tale, they wouldn't believe it any more than they'd believed Jaku when he'd told them, "That Army fire dude was really pounding Liz. Pumping her hard, yeah, and she moaned and screamed like a bitch in heat, wrapped her body around that dude like a pretzel. No lie, brah."

I especially hoped Vic didn't believe what Jaku had said about me. I wanted to ask him why Jaku was his pal, but I worried he would bristle and tell me, "None of your damn business," so I turned to my buddy Tom instead.

"Jaku's an extrovert. He can be a real crackup. Ever heard his wild tales?" Tom said. "Vic's quiet but likes a good laugh. Hell, you know this. Jaku's antics tickle his funny bone. Know what I think? Bonding with bad boy Jaku gave naïve country boy Vic a ticket into the kickass fireman community."

According to the rumor mill, the two friends had fun cruising through the nightlife, flirting with chicks—women were drawn to handsome Vic, and extroverted Jaku could be entertaining—and bar hopping, though Vic wasn't much of a drinker. But an ex-swabby nicknamed The Skipper liked to booze it up with good-time Jaku. The grapevine said the two enjoyed drunken good times together.

"Jaku might not be the sharpest axe on the truck," Tom said, "but Vic and The Skip and some of the others get a big kick out of his party-animal side. Too bad it's mirrored by a dark side." Tom didn't think Vic recognized that side at all.

I wondered if Jaku secretly felt jealous because his pal's movie-star looks attracted women. Publicly he told the guys, "Lucky for me, Vic's a chick magnet. Luckier yet, he don't go for fast wahines." He slapped his ample belly. "Me, on the other hand . . ."

Jaku acted out for his fireman audience how sometimes, when one of Vic's bevy of admirers got soused on the whiskey sours Jaku plied her with, she lowered her sights until they fell on the heartthrob's devilishly-charming pal. "Ooh, doggies! The bitch rubbed me raw," he would brag, swiveling his hips, and the firemen would laugh.

Jaku's stories usually contained at least one nugget of truth, which he embellished so he could thrust himself into the limelight. With me, it was that an Army fire captain was visiting. With Vic, I hoped it was that he steered clear of fast women, although I heard he'd succumbed once. Rumor had him and Jaku soused when an inebriated woman who worked in the chow hall kitchen came on to Vic. Jaku persuaded her to count him in, and the three of them ended up in a ménage à trois. When Jaku became abusive, Vic pried him from the woman and let her escape. She fled the islands on the following day.

I figured the three were consenting adults, but I thought the woman must have been sloppy drunk or a masochist to say yes to sex with two drunks. News of the threesome had me thinking, *Wow, Vic and Jaku are thick as thieves*, but it didn't lower my high regard for Vic. I hoped he would continue to think me amusing rather than weird because I preferred reading metaphysical books like *Seth Speaks* to watching TV shows during slow times like the other dispatchers. Some of the firemen thought I was a space case after I answered their question, "Who is Seth?" with "He's an energy essence who has completed the reincarnation cycle and is no longer focused in physical reality."

My weirdness became a topic for gossip with the firemen. Some of the guys began singing Golden Earring's theme song from the "The Twilight Zone" when I walked by. Others, noticing my habit of piling salad on my plate, would yell, "Look out guys! Better hit the salad bar before Reincarnated Rabbit gets there."

By the time 1982 rolled around, curiosity about the new dispatcher passed, and they left me alone to read my weird books. That was fine by me. I liked most of the guys well enough to make small talk, to ask the fathers among them, "How's the wife and kids?" To ask the Casanovas why only one woman had called for them lately rather than the usual three. But the firemen I enjoyed talking to more were the ones taking history, literature or philosophy classes. Our conversations sometimes took me back to college days when ideas were meat and bread. I missed those salad days, when my world spun around exciting intellectual possibilities.

What I craved far more than stimulating ideas, however, was to cherish and be cherished by a happy, kind man I could laugh with and confide in. I fantasized about a special someone who would shower me with affection and attention, want to be with me exclusively, and would never dream of dumping me for another woman.

* * *

From January 1982 onward, I increasingly looked forward to coming to work when Vic was on duty. I hoped neither of us would be tied up with alarms all night, and that he'd pop into the alarm room and chat with me.

For the next thirteen months, Vic and my friendship progressed in a slow and steady, enjoyable and relaxed fashion. When we were alone, simply talking, I felt like a human firefly, all lit up with joy.

One night in February of 1983, I was listening to his growing-up-in-the-country stories, him telling me how he felt free as a bird on the wing riding his motorcycle through the Pennsylvania forests. I was thinking I knew how he felt back then because that's how I felt in his presence, free from my usual negative self-talk, when he stopped talking and stared at me with those azure eyes of his. Finally, he said, "You sure know how to listen."

The red airfield control tower phone rang, and I don't remember if my heart pounded from that or from Vic's words as I dispatched the emergency and he ran to his truck. I do remember I floated on the good feeling from Vic's words for weeks, playing them over in my mind as I daydreamed between alarms. But I also replayed Tom's warning about Vic running from women who chase him. *Don't fall for Vic*, I told myself. *You can't risk losing his friendship, or losing Billy. And then there's Vic's shadow, Jaku the jerk.*

* * *

Having time to read and daydream most nights was one of the main reasons I liked shift work. On a quiet night in March 1983, it struck me that the central fire station was a microcosm of larger society. There were the Monday through Friday folks—fire inspectors and chiefs (the white shirts), the extinguisher shop guys, and secretaries with their 8 to 5 normalcy. During daylight hours, firemen (the blue shirts) also participated in that world, drilling, training, and following daily work routines.

After the day workers dispersed, firemen and night shift dispatchers like me inhabited a different world. It was a less structured, more downtime world, where the firemen could do pretty much whatever they liked. Many of them played twilight volleyball on the sand court outside, played cards, or watched the large-screen TV from recliners in the combination community/dining room. Others lifted weights, rode stationary bikes, ran on treadmills in the weight room, read, talked story, studied in the front office, or took naps in the bunkrooms.

The freedom the firemen enjoyed presented an opportunity for a criminal as well. A sneak thief cased the station and ripped off unwary firemen under cover of night. Stolen wallets and rifled-through cars and lockers were the norm until the guys got wise and locked up their possessions.

The guys figured the thief for one of their own because no intruder was spotted, but this couldn't be proven since no one was ever caught. I suspected Jaku. After all, he was a liar so why not a thief as well? But even when I turned the lights down low so I could peer outside through the one-way glass, I never saw anyone other than a sleepy fireman stumbling toward the bathroom.

Chapter 2

April 1983 through July 1984

Vic and I sometimes traded good-natured insults. On a sticky night in April, during the swing shift from 4 p.m. to midnight, he sat at the back desk and "talked story" with me between routine phone calls about fire checks and club closings.

I admitted missing a creative writing exam because I'd spaced out the date. "Like my mammy used to say, ain't no fool like an educated fool," Vic snickered.

I retorted, "Your mammy wears combat boots and your Italian brain is so untutored you probably think Dom Perignon was a Mafia boss."

"Don't upset me," he frowned. "Only an educated fool would fail to see I'm a righteous dude."

I pouted. "Educated fool?"

He smirked and nodded.

"My mama didn't raise no fools, educated or otherwise." I dared to add, "I see you clearly, dude."

He looked puzzled, then embarrassed. "Gotta go," he muttered, and fled.

You idiot. What are you trying to do, chase him away for good?

I worried during his next five shifts until he stopped by the alarm room, grinning and asking, "What's happening, Miss E as in English?"

"Not much, GL," I said, trying not to look deliriously happy to see him.

Vic wasn't into book learning and writing like me. He was into giving, and he liked for his friends to shine. He coined my *Miss English* nickname, and it pleased him when the chief called me his *Walking Dictionary*. But he didn't like the firemen asking me to tutor them without offering to pay.

"Don't let them impose on you, Snake," he said. "Tell them they'll get what they pay for."

I listened, bartering my services for promises of unlimited bathroom breaks.

When my tutoring helped firemen pass the English classes required for a Fire Science degree, thus bettering their chances for promotion, Vic high-fived me. "Right on, Language Lizzy," he would say.

For himself, Vic had no interest in competing for a promotion. He figured becoming a captain would force him to give up driving his beloved Ramp 7 solo. "I don't want no slow yoyo holding me back or hanging me up," he would say.

"Slow yoyo?" I teased.

"You'd best behave," he frowned, "or I'll hang YOU up."

I gave him my best deer-in-the-headlights look. "I ain't misbehaving. I'm thinking the slow yoyo who got in your way would be pupule. That's crazy to you, haole."

* * *

I considered Greased Lightning the perfect nickname for Vic, and thought his Ramp 7 rapid response pickup truck was the perfect vehicle. Several times during his frequent F-4 fighter plane standbys, the volatile jet fuel ignited as soon as the pilots started the engines. When fires flared, Vic would smother them with foam from the enormous extinguisher bolted to his truck bed, immediately, before fire could spread to the plane. His quick responses earned him medals and the admiration of his coworkers, and saved the Air Force millions of dollars.

Vic refused to attend award ceremonies honoring him. "He doesn't give a rat's ass—excuse me, Liz—about the glory," said Mighty Mite, a short, strong man who lifted weights with Vic. "Did you know he built up his cut physique with light weights and endless reps?"

"No." But it didn't surprise me. I figured Vic's disciplined weight-lifting regimen and well-honed firefighting skills were just part of who he was.

Vic's quick rescues during emergencies were a hot topic for the grapevine. On a rainy August afternoon in 1983, my pal Tom asked me, "Ever hear about Vic and the hot brakes emergency on a cargo plane, a few months before you graced us with your presence?"

I hadn't heard, so Tom filled me in. "Vic was on the scene, standing by his truck. A hundred yards away, Lino was crouched down, his back turned toward one of the plane's wheels after he'd checked it for hot brakes. They weren't hot, and the emergency had just been secured."

I knew firefighters checked the brakes by feeling them; sort of like walking up to a bomb and touching it to see if it's going to explode. And I knew, when a hot brakes emergency was called in, the pilot released the brakes, not wanting them to be engaged because, when they were, they transmitted high heat.

"The plane's engine power must have been set too high because the plane started rolling backward," Tom said. "Vic saw what was happening. He yelled but the engine roar ate up his words."

"Oh god! What did he do?"

"Well, he figured he wouldn't have time to sprint the 100 yards or so and push Lino out of the way before the wheel crushed him. So he grabbed a chock, slid it with great force across the ground, and started running."

"What's a chock?" I asked.

"A wooden wedge the guys carry in their trucks. The chock hit the tire straight on. It set up just enough resistance to make the plane roll forward a tad before resuming its backward roll."

"Hit it straight on from 100 yards?"

Tom nodded.

"Incredible," I said.

"Indeed. The guy could have been a pitcher. Anyway, it gave him the time he needed to reach Lino and shove him out of the wheel's way mere seconds before he would have turned into Flat Stanley."

I laughed, picturing Flat Stanley of storybook fame. One thing I enjoyed about the firemen was the humor they managed to find in every scenario.

"It's like Vic's got exceptional peripheral vision," Tom said. "He might be focused on a C-5's hot brakes, but he's also keenly aware what each of the guys are up to and who might be in jeopardy. Ever hear about him saving Bob's life during the fire at the fuel tank farm?"

I hadn't. I remembered that inferno, though. Remembered thinking, *oh my god* when I'd seen the billowing black smoke blot out the blue sky as I drove to Fort Craig one afternoon in August 1981, a month before I transferred to Whaler. As the entire fleet of Whaler fire trucks raced, sirens blaring, to the huge fuel tank fire, I dispatched an Army fire truck to stand by at their station.

Back then, Vic manned the turret, a powerful nozzle, on the roof of the enormous P-2 fire truck. At 13 feet wide and 33 feet long, with a 2,300-gallon water tank and 200-gallon foam tank, the P-2 was the Air Force's most formidable airfield firefighting weapon. From his high post, Vic could shoot a foam/water mixture at 1,000 gallons per minute for a distance of 175-200 feet for two minutes before the foam ran out.

When I asked Deputy Chief Bob Henderson about the incident, he said, "In those days, everybody carried radios. But we chiefs were not practiced on working a unified command."

"Meaning you didn't broadcast what was happening like you do now?"

"Exactly," Bob said. "After Vic laid a blanket of foam on top of the burning fuel in the huge tank, I didn't think to radio in that another fireman and I were walking along a pipeline at the bottom of the tank, looking for a valve to check if it was turned off."

The two men had walked into an area where the foam blanket had deteriorated. Suddenly, the fire flashed, cutting them off from exiting the same way they came in. The smoke quickly rolled over them and they couldn't see a way out.

Vic, instantly alert to what had happened, turned the turret and laid foam over the place where the two men were cut off from egress. He reopened the area so they could run out before fire singed them, filled their lungs with black smoke, or worse.

"If Vic had not been hyper aware, we would have been dead," Bob said. "So much was going on and everybody else was focusing on the tank tops, worried the fire would leap to the other tanks and the entire tank farm would ignite."

Valiant Vic, I thought, not daring to say it to his face. Afraid of chasing him away, I didn't tell him how much I admired him for his prowess on the fire scene. But even if I had, he probably would have said, "Just doing my job, Snake."

* * *

Soon after Tom told me the story about Vic saving Bob's life, Jaku started cornering me in the alarm room. I managed to avoid him when I took a dinner break by plopping my tray down at another fireman's table, but it was easy for him to trap me in my cage, as the firefighters called the dispatch office.

First he would stick his head through the door and scan the room to see if anyone sat behind the back desk or leaned against the console. If I was alone, he sauntered in and adopted what I thought of as his Mafia stance—legs spread, arms crossed across his belly, eyes gazing into space—before he dropped his pose, checked to make sure my eyes were on him, wiggled his eyebrows, and launched into a story.

I had laughed when he'd enacted fighting fires during his Vietnam days. But that was before he spread sexual lies about me. Now I fought a war of my own, battling my fear of him by focusing on his every word, intent on giving him the attention he seemed to crave. The last thing I wanted to do was offend him, lest he retaliate in some hurtful way.

The first new story Jaku acted out for me was him slapping the chief and getting away with it. "The chief scolded me for some damned thing, and threatened to terminate me," Jaku said. "I told him, 'Fool! You know who you're talking to? You terminate me, I'll terminate you!' Then I slapped him three times across his Tweety Bird face, thwap, thwap, thwap!" Jaku pantomimed forcefully backhanding the chief.

I had to smile because the chief's large, open face did look a bit like Tweety Bird's. "Later on," Jaku said, "Lino told me the chief asked him, 'Hey, Lino, Jaku's got guns, or what?' Lino told him, 'Yeah, Jaku's bad. He's got plenty guns.' Now the chief don't bother me no more."

"Wow, you are a bad dude," I said, trying to inject admiration into my voice.

I didn't know what to believe and what not to believe when Jaku told me one of his tales, so I withheld judgment until I could talk to a fireman pal and find out what actually happened. When I asked a fireman about Jaku slapping the chief, he replied, "Yep, it really did happen, and Chief didn't fire him." So I figured Jaku's story was true.

Two weeks later, in September, Jaku bragged about cutting Deputy Chief Bob's brake lines. He said he was getting even with Bob for his recommendation that Chief Green promote a fireman other than Jaku. "The fat bugger should've told Tweety Bird to hire me, no joke."

I said, "Guess Bob never crossed you again, huh?" I figured the screw bolting most people's consciences to their actions had to be broken for Jaku to admit committing such an act. Why was he telling me this? And bragging about his other crimes? I must have convinced him I was his friend for him to assume I admired his every deed no matter how dark. A spooky man, certainly, but I thought I knew how to handle him.

I confided in Deputy Chief Bob that Jaku had told me he was the one who had cut Bob's brake lines. "Nah, my stepson did it," Bob said, "when he was angry with me for insisting he go to drug counseling. Jaku's just trying to make himself look big."

Most of the firemen knew Jaku sometimes claimed credit for a crime he hadn't committed. They knew he thirsted for attention like a parched man thirsts for water. Some of the young airmen, however, idolized Jaku for being a bad ass. They longed to emulate him but didn't dare jeopardize their Air Force careers.

* * *

Vic continued to look out for me. On a cool November night, I failed to hear Mad Max quietly say, "Alarm secured, Control." Max spoke so softly I had to keep my ear close to the speaker to hear him over the radio. I had rolled my secretarial chair six feet from the console and into the doorway of the adjoining assistant chief's office, the better to talk to the guys, including Vic, sprawled out on overstuffed chairs and a tattered couch.

When Max wheeled back into the station, he yelled at me for leaving my post. "From here on out, you will stay in the alarm room at all times," he barked. All I could do was nod and tremble at his unexpected anger. I did not think I had left my post, and I figured he was the one to blame for talking so quietly I couldn't hear him. Still, I shook like a dog at the vet.

After Max stomped out, I noticed Vic's eyes had darkened with distress. How comforting to have a friend in the station.

Afterwards, when Max was on duty and I forgot to stay close to the microphone, Vic would don an exasperated expression and say, "Better get back in your cage. We don't want that man who flunked anger management training yelling at you again, do we?"

"No, we don't." I would smile at him. "Thanks for the reminder."

* * *

Vic and my conversations were usually lighthearted and humorous. But on a chilly night in January 1984, after dinner, Fire Captain Andy stuck his head into the dispatch office and said, "Your pal's going ballistic in the kitchen. He's got kitchen cleanup duty, and he's smashing dirty plates against the wall."

I had never seen Vic angry before. My heartbeat sped up. It slowed back down after I reminded myself, *wait a minute. I haven't done any-*

thing. Surely he's not mad at me. He soon strode into the alarm room, leaned against the doorway, crossed his arms, and scowled.

"What's wrong?" I asked him. "I heard you got a little wild in the kitchen."

His big fist pounded the console, making my radio microphone jump. "The dishes were caked with stinking food," he complained, "because some lazy ass firemen didn't bother to rinse them."

"What inconsiderate jerks," I said in my most soothing voice. "They're supposed to, and the sprayer's right there."

He scowled. "Big babies, don't even clean up after themselves. I ain't no nursemaid."

"I hear you," I said softly. "Nobody wants to clean up somebody else's mess, especially somebody like you who rinses his own plates and pulls his own weight."

He stared at me for a long moment before a hint of a smile punched dimples in his cheeks. "It's very observant you are, Lassie," he said, adopting an Irish brogue before turning away and striding out the door.

I felt elated by the compliment, flattered he would seek me out to talk to about how he felt, and delighted my words seemed to soothe him.

* * *

Five months later, Vic and I first talked about our significant others. He initiated the conversation by bringing up a disagreement with his girlfriend. *Wow*, I thought, *he trusts me enough to talk about her.* I hoped I could now share some of my relationship problems with him as well.

Vic had mentioned dating a hairdresser named Molly a few times, going to the beach or movies with her, and her moving in with him six months after they met. He didn't say much about her afterward until the fabric of their relationship started to rip.

That morning in June 1984, a heavy downpour splattered the taxi way beyond the airfield truck stalls. I'd been at Whaler for two years and ten months.

Looking scrubbed and shaved, and smelling of Ivory soap, Vic rested his elbows on the back desk and peeled a Kona orange—dark on the outside, sweet inside. We talked about Fred, a henpecked fireman whose wife made him brush the cat's teeth, and how Fred tried to avoid home chores by volunteering for overtime every chance he got.

"Why doesn't Fred tell her to let the vet do it?" I asked.

Vic shrugged. "He needs to grow a backbone, speak his mind. Pussyfooting around ain't no good way to live."

"You're right," I said, wishing I wasn't so timid about speaking up.

Vic bit into a section of orange and extended some slices to me. The sweet taste exploded in my mouth. I reached out for more, and he handed me the last juicy slice.

"Take me now." Vic pointed at his chest. "I got no problem saying no. Take my girlfriend Molly. I poured a can of oil on top of her car."

Oh no. Maybe he's more like Jaku than I thought. "Why?" I asked.

"She borrowed a hundred bucks, said she'd give it back on payday. Payday rolls around. No dough. I say, 'Where's the green?' She says, 'You make more money than me. What's a hundred bucks?' I say, 'Enough to cover what I'm going to do to your car if you don't pay me back by Friday.' She laughed, said, 'You'll get over it.'"

"Molly must not know you well," I said, "to think you'd roll over for that."

He frowned. "She pissed me off."

"She ought to apologize, promise not to break a promise again."

He nodded. "Yep, that's what she ought to do. That's what you would do. Am I right, Snake? Apologize if you did wrong?"

My face flushed. "If I thought I'd done wrong. Maybe she doesn't. Maybe she was low on dough?"

"Yep. Low down, too. She comes bopping into my pad with . . . ," he imitated a woman's voice and gestures, ". . . three totally cool outfits from Liberty House."

"One of those shop-until-you-drop types?"

He lowered a corner of his mouth. "Yeah. On my money."

"Still, I'm surprised at you, doing such a thing."

"Yeah?" He rubbed his chin and looked embarrassed.

How cool. Vic listens to me! I wished Billy would, and I wondered why lovers stopped hearing each other, and if there was any way to fix this.

After a long pause, Vic said, "You're right, Snake. It was beneath me, and not fair to Molly. But she tried to take advantage of me."

"That was wrong of her." *Maybe Vic's a little like me. Maybe it's hard for him to speak up about stuff he doesn't know how to deal with. Maybe it's easier to pour oil on your lover's car than figure out how to communicate.*

"The thing is, people know you're a . . . ," I searched for a more masculine word than pussycat, ". . . nice guy."

"I know it. I don't like it!" He banged the desk with his fist, making my microphone jump.

"Getting even doesn't sound like you, though," I said. "It sounds more like something Billy would do." *Or Jaku,* I thought but didn't say.

"Oh?" Vic raised an eyebrow. "Like, how?"

"Billy yells when he thinks someone's disrespecting him. When it's the boss, Billy gets fired. Then he's broke and I lend him money until the next job. He tries hard to pay me back but . . . you got upset about a hundred bucks? Try two thousand."

I didn't realize I was talking loudly until Vic said softly, "You all riled up?"

I nodded and took a deep breath. "Yesterday he got fired from an occupational therapist job. I spent hours helping him write his resume."

"Good of you to help your old man." Vic rubbed his chin between thumb and forefinger. "But do you really want to keep on like this?"

"If I don't we'll be out on the street," popped out. *Lighten up,* I thought, and added, "He just sold his car or I could've tried the oil thing. Would've gotten his attention. Gotten me killed, too."

Vic laughed and shook his head. "You're right about the oil thing being immature. I'll apologize to Molly, clean up her car." He looked at me for a long moment before saying hesitantly, "Uhh . . . if you ever need it," he patted his shoulder, "my shoulder is . . . well, it's strong enough for you to lean on."

"Thanks." I swallowed hard.

He stood. "But now I've got to put it to the wheel, so . . ." He started a slow mosey toward the door, "catch you later."

The room felt empty with Vic gone. I wished some of his self-assurance would rub off on me so I wouldn't worry that speaking my mind would drive Billy away. And I wished I didn't worry about appearing to chase Vic and driving him away. And I wished I didn't have to pretend to be Jaku's friend so he wouldn't stab me in the back.

Come to think of it, I wasn't talking straight to the three guys who impacted my life the most. I was fed up with feeling like I had to squelch my voice, but didn't know how to change.

* * *

During a slow swing shift in the middle of June, a month after Vic's girlfriend shorted him a hundred bucks, I was telling him about my upcoming trip to visit my parents in the mainland.

He rubbed his chin. "Molly moved back to L.A."

I hoped the phones wouldn't ring so we could talk for a while. "Because of the oil thing?"

"Nah. She rearranged my apartment. I told her she should have asked first."

"Well, yeah."

I wondered why lovers stopped talking to each other. On the previous day, Billy had answered, "I'm not in the mood," when I asked him if we could talk about us. Feeling discounted stung. Part of me wanted to run away, but another part swallowed hard and tried to rationalize the hurt away. I told myself it was just a male-female disconnect, with Billy needing to withdraw, and me needing a more communicative guy.

I asked Vic, "What did Molly say?"

Vic imitated a woman's high voice. "You don't like it? But it looks so chic now."

I laughed. "Chic, huh? What did you say?"

"Please put everything back where it was. This pissed her off." He shrugged and turned his palms up. "She told me I had no style, and phoned a hair salon in California, and got her old job back."

"Wow. I'm sorry, Vic. I know it hurts when a relationship goes south." I dropped the corners of my mouth in an attempt to look sad.

He made a funny face that made me smile. "I'm cool. First she keeps my green, then she turns my styling pad into girly chic. Enough already."

I wished I felt as secure as Vic to assert myself, and worried because Billy had seemed so far away lately. Was our relationship in its death throes, too?

* * *

A month later, in July 1984, Billy got fired from his substitute teaching job after arguing with a haole principal. On the following day, the landlord kicked him out of our tiny apartment for yelling at a neighbor. The only affordable place he could find on his own was a rundown, roach-infested studio in Chinatown. He hated it.

Slipping easily into the role of rescuer, I offered to loan him money until he found another job and we could afford a place together. I was scrubbing out his rusty refrigerator when he pulled me into a chair beside him and grabbed my hand. He said he'd been thinking hard about his situation.

"Miss Mizzu," he said. Mizzu, his nickname for me, for my Missouri roots. "You're a smart lady. Smart enough to see I ain't making it here on Oahu."

Instantly, my heart ached. Unable to speak, I just stared.

"I've got to get away," he said. "Things are too heavy for me now. My cousin on Maui offered me to stay with him."

My abandonment issues rose up like ghosts to choke me. The ground crumbled beneath my feet and I tumbled into despair. Billy wrapped a muscular arm around my shoulder, and held me as I cried.

The following day, my friend Carey and I sat at her kitchen table.

"I lent him money and helped him edit his term papers so he could earn a degree, find a good job. I did everything I could to up the ante he'd find me indispensable, want to work things out with me."

"Why'd you think you had to bribe Billy by doing him favors?" Carey poured me more tea.

I stirred in honey. "Maybe, to make him so happy he'd decide to stick around. So I wouldn't have to hurt like I do now."

"I'm sorry. Anything I can do to help?" She squeezed my hand.

I squeezed her back. "Talking helps. Billy and I can't really talk, not like you and me. He's leaving. We've been together for eight years. I'm scared."

"I always thought you could do better than Billy," Carey said. "Sometimes you have to let go."

"Yeah, that's what my mind says. Let go." My voice broke. "But my heart gives itself completely, and when I try to take it back, it tears, and tells me love's supposed to last. Then my mind says, 'That means it wasn't really love.' I feel split. It's so hard."

Sorrow made sleeping more than a few hours a night impossible.

A week later, on a steamy Monday night in August, Billy flew away. "I'll write," he muttered.

"I'll write back," I promised.

He said he might return. "I'm sorry to hurt you, Miss Mizzu." He stroked my cheek. "You're the best. You've been good to me." Then he was gone, the door slamming behind him.

The loud sound hung like a shroud as dust shimmered in the beams of sunlight angling through the jalousie windows. Then it faded away. Then my sobs shattered the silence.

Thankfully, I was on break day. At least I wouldn't have to face the firemen with eyes crimson from crying. My habit was to present myself and Billy as a happy couple, even when we fought. I would continue the deception with him gone.

Vic knew Billy and I had issues about money and Billy's temper. Should I tell Vic? If I did, I would swear him to secrecy. The last thing I needed was for someone odious like Jaku, who fancied himself a hot lover, to think I was up for grabs. No, I wouldn't even tell Vic.

I wrapped ice cubes in paper towels and pressed them to my eyes. The cold towels cooled them, but the tears kept flowing and my eyes stung. I would have lots of time to think about what I would and wouldn't say, since I wouldn't be cooking for Billy, or going to the beach or movies. Or swimming, or hiking with him, or making love, or anything at all.

I left the lights off when night darkened my living room. Midnight arrived before I fell asleep.

Around 2 a.m., a dream startled me awake. Knowing how easily dreams dissolve, I grabbed lined yellow paper and a red pen from my bed stand and scribbled before falling back asleep.

When I awoke the next morning, I had a vague recollection of Jaku in my apartment, and a muscular, disembodied arm coming through the living room window, and a hand grabbing me on the shoulder with a warm and reassuring touch.

I figured the hand and arm belonged to Billy, and the dream was telling me he still cared, and would come back and work things out with me, and kick Jaku's ass if he bothered me.

Comforted, I lay back down and fell asleep.

Chapter 3

August 14, 1984 through February 13, 1985

THE RAINY NIGHT after Billy left, I walked home from a grocery store a few blocks away, something I'd often done when he walked with me through our ghetto-like neighborhood. An enormous, ragged man yelled at me from across a busy street, dodged cars, and ran toward me. I sprinted to the vacant lot behind my apartment building and hid behind thorny hale koa bushes, my heart thumping, until the guy shuffled by, talking to himself.

Billy's not here to look out for me now, I thought, and resolved not to walk alone through dark streets at night again.

Nor would I make myself a target for the Casanovas at work who thought a woman living alone was fair game. Or for Jaku, who'd met muscular Billy and knew Billy could kick his ass if he bothered me. When someone asked about Billy, I said he was temporarily working in construction on Maui, saving money to bring home to me.

At first, I told only my two best girlfriends Billy was gone. Carey said, "You gave it your best shot. Time to say, 'Bye, bye, Billy,' and move on." But I couldn't let go, not yet. I missed having someone to come home to, and the good times we'd shared.

Julie told me, "God never closes a door without opening another." Maybe so, but it wasn't open now. I ached with loneliness. My shopping cart looked empty without Billy's steak, poi and beer nestled next to my broccoli, brown rice and chicken. My tiny apartment seemed cavernous and quiet. I cried and cried, easing my sore eyes with eye drops and ice cubes before crying some more.

***

A few weeks after Billy left, my car was in the shop for repairs. Jaku overheard me asking for a ride home, and interrupted me with, "How come you never ask me? Come! I'm giving Greg a ride, too, and I've only got to make one stop. I live just around the corner from you, did you know?"

I shook my head even though I knew exactly where Jaku lived. Since he and I wouldn't be alone in the car, and since I didn't dare refuse, I said yes. The last place I'd expected his stop to be was the south side of the barbed-wire-topped fence surrounding the penitentiary. "I'm going to talk to the brothers," he told Greg and me. "They wait for me."

Jaku parked his black Toyota in an empty parking lot choked with thick dry weeds groping through broken asphalt. He walked to the fence to face two big, dark-skinned men on the other side, their thick fingers hooked through the metal fence's diamond-shaped openings, their eyes staring out at freedom.

Jaku and the men spoke in low voices for a good fifteen minutes. A whistle blew. The prisoners unhooked their fingers and slowly walked away.

"Those guys are victims of society," Jaku philosophized, wriggling his eyebrows between curses as he cut in and out of slow lanes of going-home traffic. I promised myself I would catch the bus next time. "They're just like me or you. When you poor, you out the door. They treat you like trash when you got no cash."

He went on about his underprivileged prison friends. Greg and I withdrew into our audience mode, throwing in a word of agreement now and then.

When Jaku pulled into the parking lot in front of my fourplex, he asked, "You live where Jason used to live, yeah, Liz?" He pointed to the upstairs, northernmost unit.

"Yes." I figured he knew, so why lie? "Me and Billy," I added. The firemen had told me Jaku peered through high-powered binoculars at people's windows, hoping for some titillating views. Billy and I had kept the curtains drawn, but I wondered if, from the walkway above his apartment a few blocks away, his binoculars gave him a view of the stairway to our front door.

Uneasy, I thanked Jaku for the ride. I resolved to ask the landlord again to install a deadbolt in the front door.

* * *

Several weeks later, I was able to admit things hadn't been good between Billy and me for a long time and, while fidelity and commitment were important, without communication they just weren't enough.

As the serenity of Billy being gone grew on me, so did my crush on Vic. A few weeks later, I decided to confide in Vic that Billy was living on Maui permanently. After all, Vic had confided in me about Molly moving back to California.

"I thought Billy was coming back," Vic said.

"I told everyone he was, but he's not. Promise you won't tell a soul, especially Jaku."

Vic looked startled. "Why not?"

I frowned. "The last thing I need is Jaku spreading lies about me again."

"Aww, nobody believes the sawed-off, gabby guy. But . . . okay . . ." He crossed his heart. "Mum's the word."

"Thanks," I said, confident Vic was the sort who kept his word.

* * *

In early September, Vic underwent surgery to repair the deviated septum in his nose. His fireman pal Tony, Tony's girlfriend Annie, and I visited him in his sub-zero hospital room. Tony handed him a Playboy magazine and Annie a box of chocolate-covered macadamia nuts. I gasped at the mass of blue and purple bruises above and below the white bandages spanning his nose.

"It's not as bad as it looks," Vic said. I set a small potted plant with fuzzy purple flowers in a plastic pot on his bed stand. He smiled. "A plant, huh?"

"I thought about cut flowers," I said, "but they die so quickly. This plant will grow." I wished I had brought him something more hip.

He said, "It's a cool plant, Snake." Since he'd ridden his bike to the hospital and had no way to take the plant home, he asked if I would drop it by his pad in a week or so. Of course I said yes.

He wrote his phone number on a paper napkin. "You have a phone?" I asked. "Didn't you tell the chief you don't?"

He nodded. "I only give the number to my friends. I don't want the chief bothering me when I'm off duty with some petty bullshit he could ask me about at work."

"Your guilty secret is safe with me." I decided bringing him a plant had been a brilliant move, giving me a chance to visit him away from the fire station and Jaku.

Tony asked if Jaku had stopped by. "Not yet," Vic admitted, "but he said he would."

Tony's eyes caught mine. We both figured Jaku wouldn't show, figured his circuits weren't wired to think about anyone's needs but his own.

When we stood up to leave, Annie kissed Vic's cheek, Hawai'ian style. She paved the way for me and I happily followed, touching my cool lips to his hot cheek, something I would never have dared to do had I been alone with him.

The following Saturday, on September 1, I phoned Vic, but his line was busy for so long I grew impatient, grabbed the plant, and drove the two blocks to his place. He answered my knock with a telephone receiver pressed to his ear, his eye sockets still purple and blue. Grinning, he motioned me inside, and pointed at his brown and white plaid couch. I sat and looked around.

His neatly organized studio apartment was home to hundreds of phonograph records, lined up in wooden crates against the east wall. On top of the crates, dozens of eight-track reel-to-reel tapes were stacked in tidy rows inside plastic cubes, on top of which rested a tape player, stereo receiver, and record player. I spotted my favorite albums among his wide assortment of jazz, blues, rock and roll, and big band music, and thought he had terrific taste in music.

He had a taste for the beautiful as well. A delicate, four-sided, three-tiered shell chandelier hung between the couch and stereo equipment. Light from the naked bulb dangling in the middle reflected on hundreds of tiny white shells, their sparkle reminding me of hot beach sand shimmering in the sun.

"Well, got to go now, somebody came over," he told the caller. He listened for a moment before adding, "Yeah, me too."

Words of love? Was it possible Molly wasn't gone for good? I hoped not. At least she was gone now, and I was here, and Vic was smiling at me.

When he finished his phone conversation, I raised my eyebrows.

"Molly forgot her curtains," Vic said. "I told her I'd mail them."

Relieved, I said, "They're chic ones, no doubt."

He laughed. "How about some music?"

"Sure."

"Some Neil Diamond for you, I think."

"How did you know I like Neil? He's one of my favorites."

"I just figured he'd be your type."

Sensuous music filled the room. Here I was, hanging with Vic, and he was playing romantic melodies for me. I pinched myself; it hurt. Yep, this was real.

"I think I've got a black thumb." He placed the plant on the window sill. "My prior plants died but I'll try to remember to water this one."

He proudly showed me a hanging aquarium he'd bought at Rare Discovery, a pricey art store in Honolulu. He'd stashed the aquarium on the top shelf of his walk-in closet because the only suitable spot for hanging was already occupied by his gravity boots bar. Molded from rough, unpainted ceramic, the aquarium was shaped like a porthole with thick pieces of round glass embedded in two parallel facing sides.

The aquarium struck me as a fitting symbol for Vic—one of a kind, a piece of work, a heavy weight. One tug on the thick rope hanger told me I couldn't budge it, but he easily hoisted it up to its storage place on the top shelf of his walk-in closet.

Although Vic couldn't afford many luxuries on his fireman's salary, his record and tape collection, chandelier, aquarium, and plush double futon bed were first rate.

"Want something to eat, Liz?"

"Sure." Too excited to be hungry, I wasn't about to say no to his good-host offer.

His cupboard was nearly bare, so he rustled me up a meal made with Hamburger Helper. I sat across from him at his wooden spool table.

"Tastes yummy," I said. "I only see you eat yogurt, papaya and tuna at the station. No greasy chow hall food for you. Is that why you've got so much get up and go?"

The dimples in his cheeks deepened. "I want to stay healthy, hang around for the long haul. Like my old man. He's 63 now, in great shape. Still works out. Want to see a picture of him later?"

"Yes."

When I finished eating, Vic invited me to play checkers on his king-sized futon because his wooden spool table was too small for the checkerboard. I faced him on my belly, sinking down into the thick, soft fold-up mattress.

"So comfy," I said. "My landlord's lumpy old mattress hurts my back. Think I'll save up for a futon like yours."

"My back ached before I bought this. Pricey, but you get what you pay for."

He beat me at checkers three times in a row. Then he carried a shoe box full of medals he had earned as a sergeant in Vietnam, and some photo albums, to the couch. I sat beside him as he told me what the medals stood for, pointed at snapshots of his mother and father, two sisters, and their families. He talked about them at length. When he showed me pictures of Molly, a couple of girls at the beach, and himself and Jaku at bars posing with different girls, he didn't elaborate and I didn't ask. He became loquacious again when he showed me pictures of himself in high school and his hometown in Pennsylvania.

We laughed and talked and he teased me and I teased him back and drank him in like wine and wished I did not have to remain sober. But I did not dare overstay my unannounced visit, so eventually forced myself to say, "Thanks for your hospitality. Awesome food and music, and company. Wish I didn't have to go."

Had I really said "awesome company"? My audacity amazed me. I hoped I hadn't said too much. I tried to appear self-confident as I waved and walked away.

Vic watched me from his front door. "Thanks for stopping by."

I turned around, smiling, hoping my hot face hadn't turned red. "My pleasure."

"Stop by again sometime." His blue eyes sparkled.

If lightning had struck me dead at that moment, I would have died happy.

* * *

On a Saturday night three weeks later, I drove to Vic's apartment again. Earlier in the week, I'd confided to him, "With Billy gone, I miss going to movies. I don't go because I don't like going alone."

Vic's energy had warmed the cold alarm room. A big grin creased his face. "I'd go with you to a movie sometime," he said, quite innocently.

"Really?" His words made my heart rev faster than his Chevy truck's eight-cylinder motor. I jumped on it, said, "Thanks, Vic. You're a pal. How about Saturday? I get off work at four and it's your break day."

He mumbled "sure" and practically ran out of the alarm room. Half an hour later, Tony buzzed me on the intercom. "I hear Annie and I are going to a movie with you and Vic on Saturday night."

"Oh, great." I tried to sound excited in spite of my disappointment at Vic not wanting to be alone with me. On our date, however, I appreciated Tony and Annie being there to stimulate conversation, since I was tongue-tied and nervous at actually being on a date with Vic.

We met at Vic's "stylin' pad," listened to some of his "boss sounds," talked and laughed and sipped the red Merlot he served us in frosty glasses. Then he and I headed out in his shiny red S-10 Chevy pickup truck, Tony and Annie following in their old Ford.

With Vic sitting beside me, I couldn't keep my mind on the movie. He drove me straight home afterward, shook my hand, and said he'd had a good time. "I'm gonna mosey over to Jaku's pad, down some suds, play some poker."

I hid my disappointment at him not trying to kiss me and choosing Jaku's company over mine. "I had a good time, too," I said. I hadn't really. I'd been way too nervous.

Back in my apartment, I sobbed and watched my beautiful fantasy wither. *Well,* I tried to console myself, *Vic's friendship enhances my life more than any man-woman relationship I've known. Maybe it's better this way.* But I didn't really believe it was.

Four days later, Ted Fisher, a hard-drinking fireman, strode into the alarm room. "So." He looked me up and down. "I hear you're dating firemen now."

What? How did he know? "Where'd you hear that?"

He stared. "Rumor has it you and Vic and Tony . . ." his voice trailed off.

"And Annie watched a movie together." I shrugged. "So what?"

He raised a bushy eyebrow. "Did you and Vic . . . ?" He made a circle of the thumb and index finger of his right hand, and thrust his left index finger in and out of the circle.

Stunned, I could only sputter, "You're crass." I wanted to jump up and slap him, but restrained myself.

"What's crass?" he asked, seemingly with no clue he had offended me.

"Look it up, Einstein," I hissed.

He scowled. "Actually, I don't care what you do." He stomped out the door, leaving me seething and thinking Tony must have opened his big mouth and spread the word about our double date.

The following morning, Jaku cornered me in the alarm room and quizzed me about Billy and my date with Vic. I shielded myself with lies, "Billy's moving back next month. He said he didn't mind me watching a movie with a friend."

Jaku squinted at me, as if trying to see whether I lied. I wondered if Vic had already told him the same thing, or if the two friends had spoken about it at all.

On his next shift, Jaku changed his usual routine of bragging about a crime he'd committed. Instead, he launched into a story about a boss babe he met in a bar. He said he'd bought the mini-skirted chick a couple of drinks and could tell by the way she looked at him she knew he'd do her right. "Ooh, Liz," he said, rolling his hips and staring, "I gave the *wahine* a night she ain't never gonna forget." He shrugged. "She kept calling me after, but I shined her on.'"

I wondered why Jaku's stories had changed from true crime to cruel Casanova.

* * *

Vic stopped dropping by the alarm room. Bewildered and anxious, I had a sense of dread that I'd somehow turned him off during the date. Two weeks after we saw the movie, I spotted him at the drinking fountain in the airfield truck stalls and walked over to say hello.

He frowned. "You talk too much."

I felt like the concrete beneath my feet had turned to quicksand. My breath caught in my throat. Too stunned to speak, I stared.

Vic wiped his mouth with the back of his hand, glared at me, and strode away.

The pain of Vic blaming me for something I didn't do hit me like a hard punch to my heart. I barely made it to the bathroom before my tears began to spill. I hid there until my sobs subsided and the cold water I splashed on my face washed the hot tears away. Glad the community room was empty, I hurried through it and back to the alarm room.

The relief fireman, my pal Danny, asked, "How come your eyes all bloodshot?"

"Vic . . ." I swallowed hard, "said I . . . I talk too much. But I don't . . ."

Danny speculated Vic was embarrassed by what the chief had said at roll call the prior week. "Did you hear about that?" he asked.

I shook my head. My body shook, too.

"Both shifts were there, A-shift getting off, B-shift coming on, so more than 40 guys," Danny said. "The chief said, 'There will be no fraternizing with the alarm room operators.' He looked straight at Vic, who turned red and hung his head."

Oh god. I'd probably lost Vic's friendship forever. After Danny left, I locked the door and cursed the chief for being an interfering busy body, and Tony for being a big-mouthed gossip.

The ranting made me feel better. I gave myself a pep talk, "Don't give up. Don't crawl into your shell. Find a way to tell Vic what happened."

The following Saturday, on my morning break, I spied Vic sitting alone at one of the vinyl-topped dining room tables, eating tuna and crackers. Mr. Tennyson, a fifty-something, well-read fire captain, sat at another table, working a New York Times crossword puzzle.

I caught Vic's eye and pointed at him. "There will be no fraternizing with the alarm room operators."

Tenny looked up from his newspaper. "What's fraternizing mean?" he asked.

I shook my head and tried to stop the rest of me from shaking, too. "As if you didn't know."

He raised his eyebrows. "Something kind of . . . provocative?"

"It can mean that." I smiled. "It can also mean associating with someone cordially. Like friends. Like Vic and me." I wondered if my pounding heart was loud enough to hear.

Both of them smiled back.

"Leave it to Liz the English Whiz," Vic said, waving me over.

I sat beside him, squared my shoulders and spit out, "It wasn't me who blabbed. So it must have been Tony."

Vic looked startled. He rubbed his chin with his right index finger and thumb and finally said, "I'm glad it wasn't you, Snake."

"Why didn't you ask me instead of assuming?" In spite of myself, my eyes misted up.

A sheepish look crossed his face. After a long moment he answered, "Guess I was being a chauvinist pig, figuring, you know, women like to . . . talk."

I just looked at him.

Vic thought about it for a moment. "You're right." Then, hesitantly, "I should have asked."

Relief flooded over me, but I didn't trust myself to speak lest I tear up.

"Liz . . ." his voice trailed off, "assuming made an ass out of me."

I bit my lip and blinked hard.

Vic extended his right hand, "I won't assume again."

We shook, my small cold hand warmed by his large one.

"I won't believe anything anybody says about you unless you say it's true," he added. "Promise."

I wondered what people were saying about me. "It's a deal." I tried to smile.

He didn't say another word. The tender look in his eyes was answer enough.

* * *

After mid-September, Jaku told me a new obscene story about yet another sexual conquest every day he was on duty. His stories disgusted me. Not being able to tell him to get the hell out locked me in a prison cell with him. I felt like a little mouse, and he was a big cat moving in on me.

Jaku had been telling me these stories for almost a month when he came up with one on October 15 I could not stomach. He sauntered into the alarm room, wiggled his eyebrows, and launched into a tale about this boss chick who gave him red wings. Two firemen sat in the adjoining assistant chief's office, taking it all in.

Jaku pinned me with his eyes. "Don't you think she should have told me she was on her rags before she asked me to eat her out?"

The firemen snickered.

I wanted to slap them all. Unable to contain myself, I said in a clipped voice, "I don't give a—"

At that moment, the red fire airfield emergency telephone rang. I dispatched the alarm, hot brakes on a C-5. Jaku and the others ran to their trucks. Saved by the bell indeed.

It was the final outrage. I either had to find a way to stop Jaku from annoying me, transfer out, or quit my job. I told Sergeant Maxwell, the assistant chief, "Jaku's harassing me."

"I'll kick him out of there for you." Max frowned.

"You don't understand," I whispered. "Jaku does hurtful things to people when he thinks they've crossed him.'"

He pursed his lips and shook his head. "Jaku's just a blast of hot air. He talks big but I doubt he'd really do anything."

Wanting to protect this man from Jaku's back-stabbing revenge if I could, I said, "Let me try and handle it first."

Max looked doubtful but agreed. "Remember, I'll kick him out of there if you want me to."

A few hours later, Vic sat at the station captain's desk, filling out training reports, and Jaku sat at the back desk, guitar in hand, ready to serenade me. He started telling me a sadistic, graphically pornographic story about some woman he'd supposedly had sex with.

I had decided to tell Jaku, very nicely, I'd rather he didn't tell me about his conquests, and had begun by saying, "You know, Jaku, there's something I've been meaning to ask you . . ." when Max popped into the alarm room and heard me.

He turned to Jaku and said, "Jaku, are you making a nuisance of yourself?"

Vic, seeing what was happening, slipped out the door.

"I ain't doing nothing," Jaku insisted.

Max ordered him to get out and stay out of the alarm room.

Half an hour later, one of the guys told me Max called everybody into the training room and told them he didn't want anybody annoying the ladies in the alarm room.

The moment I was alone, Jaku strode into the assistant chief's office, leaned against the alarm room door, squinted at me, and asked, "Did you say anything to Mad Max?"

The lie came easily to my lips, "No. You know how uptight Mad Max is."

Jaku nodded, seemingly convinced. I relaxed, thinking he didn't hold me responsible.

A few days later, when A-shift was on duty, Vic asked me why I'd had Jaku kicked out of the alarm room.

"Oh my god. Does Jaku know?" I asked.

Vic shook his head.

"Thank goodness." I relaxed. "Because he was totally grossing me out."

Surprise filled Vic's face. "I thought you were used to him."

I had never told Vic I believed my survival depended on hiding my true feelings from the man he thought was just a funny little guy trying to act big. I tried to explain, "I couldn't stomach it anymore. His stories make me sick. Lately I've been dreading coming to work when he's here, because I know I'll be forced to listen to another disgusting story."

Vic looked thoughtful. "Guess I didn't think how a lady would feel." His voice softened. "I understand."

* * *

I couldn't stop thinking about Vic, how heroic and funny he was. He was so very comfortable in his skin. I wished I could be more like him, with his positive attitude and high energy. Like all shy people who are secretly in love, I fantasized. I didn't dare tell Vic how I felt, but I hoped our shared emergencies, conversations, and laughter worked in my favor.

Always on the lookout for a way to connect with Vic away from work and Jaku, I found one two weeks later, on Halloween. Creating a one-of-a-kind costume for myself, I layered strips of newspaper and glue over a large balloon to form a Papier-mâché pumpkin head.

When it dried, I spray-painted the enormous inverted bowl orange and placed it over my head. Seeing out of the triangle eyes I'd hacked through the head was difficult, and the large bowl muffled my voice.

The foundation for the body of the costume was the black leotard and tights I wore to teach yoga. Over these, I tied a string of large, green crêpe paper leaves around my waist. I also tied a string of small orange balloons painted with black-marker pumpkin faces around my arms, waist and legs. Voila! Liz the Pumpkin Patch!

I hoped to win the prize for most original costume at my friend Carey's Halloween party.

On the afternoon before the festivities, I decided to try out the effect of my costume on Vic, surprise him, hopefully give him a laugh, and show off my slim figure to good advantage. I drove the one-and-a-half blocks to his place, removed the muumuu I'd worn over tights and leotard, tied on leaves and balloons, and donned my pumpkin head. As I walked up his apartment building stairs, Vic happened to be striding down, his long legs spanning three steps at a time. He stopped, stunned, at the sight of me.

I held out a paper bag. "Trick or treat!"

Through the pumpkin head's triangle eyes I saw the fear in his. "I don't have anything!" he yelled, rushing past me and down the stairs.

I pulled the mask off and called down the stairwell after him, "Vic! Wait! It's me, Liz."

A few moments later, he stuck his head around the bend in the stairs, a wide grin on his face. "I didn't recognize you. I thought you were a . . . sicko."

We sat down side by side on the landing. He laughed, squeezed my balloons, and told me it was a swell costume, all the more so because I had made it myself. We talked awhile. He said he was headed for the gym, and walked me to my car, where I removed the balloons and pulled on my muumuu.

"Oh, yeah," he said. "Guess you can't drive with balloons around your waist."

He opened my car door for me, a puzzled look on his face. "Did you come over here just to show me your costume?" he asked, the thought just occurring to him.

My heartbeat speeded up. I tried to keep my voice steady when I answered, "Yes. Aren't you flattered?"

He continued to stare as the realization settled into him. The look in his eyes changed from amused to wondering.

Feeling nervous and not wanting to appear too forward, I hastened to add, "I'm going to a party and hope to win most original costume and wanted your opinion."

He grinned. "That's cool, that's cool. My opinion is the prize for most original costume goes to . . ." he paused for a long moment, "Miss Snaky Lady Lizzy, queen of the dispatch office."

"Thanks." My cheeks burned. I hoped my face hadn't turned red.

He laughed.

I smiled all the way home, delighted my audacity had won me the prize I really wanted—a compliment from and connection with Vic.

I had just stepped out of my blue VW bug after parking in my driveway when Vic pulled in behind me in his red pickup. "Thanks for dropping by," he yelled. "You'll win hands down. What's the prize and when do we celebrate?"

I thought, *you're the prize, and we can celebrate any old time* but, tongue-tied by my crush on him, I simply shrugged and smiled. He waved and sped off in his truck.

I had planned to take a short nap before the party but instead lay on my bed, wide awake, thinking about the look in Vic's eyes and daydreaming about him looking at me the same way when he carried me over the threshold of his studio apartment on our wedding day.

* * *

Unbeknownst to me, I'd had Jaku kicked out of the alarm room on the 75th day of his trial 90-day promotion to captain. One of four eligible firefighters, he was given an opportunity to work the job after a permanent vacancy came open. Vic, satisfied to be the solo ramp truck driver, didn't try out for the job. Even though Jaku had been told his promotion was temporary until the chief decided who to select for the position permanently, he'd told the guys, "The chief's gonna pick me, hey, no joke, if he knows what's good for him."

Apparently the chief didn't know what was good for him because, a week before Jaku's temporary promotion ended, the chief promoted another firefighter permanently.

After that, Jaku mostly stayed away from me since he could no longer pass the threshold of the alarm room. Relieved that I didn't have to listen to his sex stories any longer, I worried he might hold me responsible for his not being promoted.

Jaku and I spoke again on December 30, the day before his two weeks of annual leave was scheduled to begin. I normally kept the door locked. However, during a midnight shift on a hot night, I'd propped it open because the air conditioner was broken.

As usual, I turned the lights down low to keep an eye on the station and prevent outsiders from looking in.

The last thing I expected to see was Jaku dripping sweat and slipping into the alarm room. His head turned rapidly from side to side as he peered into the corners of the darkened room, making sure no one lurked there.

"This fuckin' place pisses me off," he said. "You heard the chief promoted John?"

"No," I said, although I had. "I'm sorry."

"The chief better wise up. Or else." The red lights on the alarm panel reflected in his eyes. "I'm gonna look for another job, maybe a security guard. Tweety Bird's just using me." His red eyes gleamed. "Using you, too, Liz."

I gave Jaku no indication I did not agree with his victim fantasy.

After his two weeks of leave were over, Jaku called in sick. A month of this and the chief told him he either had to come back to work on Valentine's Day with a doctor's excuse or be fired.

I prayed he would not return. Every day he was away felt like a holiday. Without Jaku around to drag me down, my happiness soared. Vic seemed like a freer, happier man. My feelings for him blossomed like summer roses. I thought I was doing a good job of keeping them under wraps, but I couldn't hide what was happening inside of me. Something was thawing. My ice floes were cracking and melting in the sunlight of my desire. Anxiety picked at me because I didn't think Vic felt the same way. Still, I ironed my best blouses and washed my hair before heading to work when he was on shift.

I had kissed him once, on the cheek, when I visited him in the hospital. He shook my hand after our double date. He touched me again on the morning before Valentine's Day.

Vic strolled into the alarm room that morning, crossed his muscled arms across his blue fireman's shirt, and said, "I heard somebody looks mighty pretty today." He ran his gaze over my frilly white blouse, embroidered blue jeans, and the red tennis shoes I'd bought the day before. "I see it's true, Miss Red, White and Blue."

I smiled my thanks, glad he had noticed the care I'd taken to look nice. For him, but he didn't know this. At least, I didn't think he did.

"Watch this . . . I'm a stylin' dude," he said, and performed his high-stepping strut. I laughed. Dimples popped out in his cheeks and he leaned against the edge of the dispatching console.

I swiveled to face him. "Dude, your walk is so cool, I'm shivering."

He raised an eyebrow, his eyes boring into me. "Are you now?"

I nodded and hoped my face wouldn't betray me. I changed the subject. "Did you hear Squeaky during the fire last night?"

He mimicked in a shrill voice, "We've got a working fire here, Control!" Everybody ragged on Squeaky, the assistant chief whose voice shot up three octaves when confronted with a fire.

I laughed. "You sound just like him."

He rubbed his cleanly-shaved chin. "You still teaching yogurt, Snake?"

"Yep, still eating it, too."

He grinned. Then, like the sun unexpectedly shrouded by dark clouds, his smile vanished, replaced by a frown.

Vic wasn't the moody type, and I had no idea why he strode to my side, spread his fingers wide, shoved his large hands in my face and emphatically said, "Look at the size of these hands!" Then he cradled my face with them.

His fingers felt hot as fire. His azure eyes blazed unblinkingly into mine. I inhaled sharply, my heart wildly pounding. The soft touch of Vic's hands coupled with my desire for him made me tremble. Knowing Vic's propensity for humor, I decided he must be playing and I just didn't understand the game. At a loss for something witty to say, I told the truth, "Vic, you send chills up my spine."

He pulled his hands back, his eyes still burning. His voice low, he said, "Oh, stop it," and turned away.

Three quick strides took him to the tiny back window of the alarm room, where he stared at the crowded parking lot fronting the station. Without another word or a glance my way, he strode out of the room and into the fire truck stalls, leaving me to wonder at his sudden change of mood.

I have wished ten thousand times since then that I had asked him why he was moody, or that he would have turned to me instead of turning away, and told me what was coming down.

Chapter 4

Thursday, Valentine's Day 1985

A MAN WITH kaleidoscope eyes invaded my dream, screaming and pointing a rifle at me as he chased me from room to room. I locked the door behind me, and was panting with relief at escaping him when he drilled a hole in the wall and pointed the rifle at me again.

Terrified, I shot up in bed, forcing my eyes open. The luminescent numbers on the clock radio on my nightstand read 9 a.m.

"Oh god," I groaned. I had fallen asleep only half an hour earlier, my head sinking into the pillow minutes after I arrived home from working the midnight shift.

I lay back down, but pounding on my front door made me bolt back up. Tony's muffled voice came through an open window in the living room, "Wake up, Liz!"

I scrambled out of bed, pulling on shorts and a T-shirt as I hurried to the door and flung it open. "What's happening?" I squinted at him through morning sun, raindrops in his blond hair reflecting the light.

"May I come in?" Tony's hazel eyes looked like emeralds in his pale, drawn face.

I motioned him inside. He plopped down on my threadbare couch and crossed his long arms over his aloha shirt. "Jaku's place is crawling with cops," he said, "and Vic's truck is parked sideways, inside of the police tape."

"Are you kidding me?" My sleepy mind struggled to understand Tony's words.

"I wish." He swallowed hard. "I didn't want to go over there by myself."

Fully awake now, I asked, "What do you think it could be?"

Tony shook his head and ran bony fingers through his hair, again and again. "I was driving east on Mill when I spotted crime scene tape blocking off Jaku's garage." His voice broke. "Jaku lives just around the corner, did you know?"

"Yes." I shoved my feet into tennis shoes. "Do you want to drive?"

Tony shook his head. "No parking. Let's hoof it."

We bolted down the stairs leading from my second story apartment, and ran down the sidewalk, taking care not to slip on the wet concrete.

"What do you think, a drug bust?" Panting, I tried to keep up with Tony's long-legged stride. The grapevine said Jaku was a druggie, often high or low on something, and a dealer, unloading poor quality pot for primo prices at the fire station.

"But why the police barrier?" Tony scowled. "Why the God-damned barrier?" His voice shook.

Fear crept into me.

We rounded the corner onto Aluki Avenue. Across the street from a police-taped, four-car, open garage, a crowd gathered in the shade of a monkey pod tree. Everyone strained to see what the uniformed cops and men wearing black jackets and slacks were doing in the garage, but Vic's red truck, parked sideways in front of Jaku's black Toyota, blocked the view.

I asked a woman, "What happened?"

"I heard it was a suicide," she said.

"What!? No way!" I didn't realize I was yelling until I noticed people staring at me.

Tony grabbed my arm. We hurried across the street to where a tall, muscular Samoan police lieutenant stood street-side of Vic's truck.

"They're firemen," I said. "Vic Lazzarini and Jaku Cardoza. We work with them."

He narrowed his eyes at us and remained silent.

Desperately, I persisted, "Tony here's a firefighter. I'm a dispatcher."

After a long pause, the lieutenant said, "There was an argument."

Unable to speak, I stared. The sun slipped behind a cloud. I slipped deeper into fear. The rain stopped.

The cop continued to squint at us. After another pause, he said, "One of them was shot. Dead."

"Which one?" I tried to squelch the voice in my mind that already knew.

"Well . . . we're not supposed to say. But if you work with them . . ." His voice trailed off.

"We do! Can't you tell us?" Nausea washed over me. "Is it Jaku . . . I mean Christian . . . Cardoza?" I prayed, *Please, God. Let it be Jaku.*

The lieutenant remained silent. Tony asked, "Is it the man who drove the red truck? Is it Vic Lazzarini?"

The cop stared at us. I wanted to yell, "Speak NOW," and sink my nails into his bull neck until he said, "No, it isn't Vic." But he didn't speak, he only nodded, at Tony, not me. "Mr. Cardoza claims Mr. Lazzarini came at him with a gun, claims he shot him in self-defense."

"They were friends, Lieutenant," Tony said. "They hung out together."

"It's too bad friends will fight." The lieutenant looked at us appraisingly. "Would the two of you be willing to make a written statement?"

"Vic's . . . dead?" The words caught in my throat. Impossible. He'd joked with me only yesterday. Dead? Blood drained from my head. I nearly fainted.

Tony wrapped a warm arm around my shoulder. "Oh god, Liz."

I tried to speak but only a whisper squeezed through my lips. "Did you know I was crazy about Vic?"

Tony nodded but I don't think he heard me. I asked the lieutenant, "Is Jaku still around? Will he read what I write?"

"No, he's in police custody, ma'am." The lieutenant glanced at the men milling around in Jaku's garage. "Wait here."

He ducked under the black and yellow tape of the police barrier and walked into Jaku's garage. Moments later, a short, portly man wearing a blue aloha shirt and black slacks hurried toward us. He introduced himself as Detective Randy Grabowski, handed us forms, said to fill them out and give them to the lieutenant. He disappeared back into the garage.

I rested the paper against Vic's red truck cab and wrote, "Jaku is a liar and a thief. Don't believe a word he says. Vic was a good man, honest and brave. I can't believe he had a gun."

Tony wrote something brief. Ambulance sirens wailed in the distance, softly at first, then screaming.

"Coming for Vic's body." Tony swallowed hard. "I've seen a lot of bodies, but this is one body I don't want to see."

"Me, neither." I hadn't thought about Vic's body, hidden from us inside the barrier, probably outlined in chalk on the garage floor. But now I thought about his flesh atrophying in a moldy coffin and almost stopped breathing.

Tony and I walked slowly up the hill we'd hurried down before. My legs felt as heavy as marble pillars. *Only his body's dead. His spirit's probably hovering, wondering what the hell happened.* I grabbed Tony's hand. "Oh, Tony. Our Vic is dead."

Tony sandwiched my small hand between his long bony ones. "He liked you a lot. He told me so."

"Thanks for telling me." I tried to smile.

Tony phoned the fire chief from my place. "I'm at Liz's. We just walked back from Jaku's and . . ." He paused. "Just now?" Another pause. "Echo that, Chief."

He hung up the phone. "A detective called the chief. He's all broken up. How about you? Want me to stay awhile?"

"Isn't Annie waiting?"

Tony nodded. "I can call and tell her I'll be late."

"Thanks. You're a pal. But I'll be okay. I'll try to crash."

He hugged me, said, "Get some sleep," and hurried out the door.

With Tony gone, my tiny apartment seemed huge and empty. My body felt numb, as if my nerve endings had fallen asleep. The most comforting thing I could think of to do was kneel and pray, "Dear God, I'm sure Jaku murdered Vic. Please, please, send me a dream, tell me what the argument was about."

I believed I could get the answer in my sleep. In the past, I'd had vivid dreams whose magical mindscapes revealed truths hidden from my conscious mind. My habit of forcing myself awake and jotting my dreams down allowed me to capture them before they vanished like mist in the light of my waking consciousness. Plopping down on my bed, I fell into a dreamless sleep.

When I awoke, it was night. The horror of Jaku killing Vic swept over me. Surrounded by shadows dappled with light, I noticed the pitch-blackness was alleviated only by a naked yellow light bulb dangling from the outside walkway roof. The bulb swayed in the stiff wind, casting barely enough illumination for me to move from bed to couch without stumbling. *Oh, Vic. Where are you now?*

I reached for the phone, punched in my friend Candy's phone number, and told her about the killing. "Can I come over? I don't want to be alone."

"Of course." Candy's voice was kind. "Rob and I will wait dinner for you. We can eat and talk."

Still in the dark, I locked the jalousie windows, slung my purse over my shoulder, and reached for the doorknob.

The loud slap of shoes on the concrete stairs leading up to my second story apartment made me retract my hand. Long tortuous shadows, backlit by the swaying yellow bulb, slid across the drawn white curtains.

I sank down on the couch and waited silently, hoping the shadows would disappear. But they continued to ripple across the billowing curtains. Did they belong to Jaku's criminal connections? How had he found out what I'd told the cops so quickly? Except for my hammering heart, the silence dragged on. I hoped the thugs would go away if they thought no one was home.

I nearly fainted when a loud banging on the front door was immediately followed by an authoritative voice saying, "Police!" Springing up from the couch, I flung the door open.

Detective Randy from the crime scene stood beside a tall, wiry Japanese man with gray eyes. He introduced himself as Detective Jet Yamasato, showed me his badge, and said, "This is my partner, Randy Grabowski."

We shook hands all around. "Hello again," I said to Randy.

"We've met," Randy told his partner.

"You're Lizbeth?" Jet asked.

"Please call me Liz."

"Call us Jet and Randy."

They squeezed past me, their big bodies filling my small living room. For the moment, I felt safe because The Law was present.

They sat on the couch. I faced them in an overstuffed chair, and answered Randy's question about why I showed up at the scene. Jet pulled my statement from a folder and scanned it.

"You're a dispatcher?" Jet asked. "You worked with these two firemen?"

I nodded.

"Four shots to the body at close range," he hissed. "With that kind of rage, the man's a menace."

"Four times!" I whispered. "At close range?" I shuddered. "Really? Four times?"

Jet and Randy stared at me silently.

I swallowed hard and took several deep breaths before continuing. "I've been afraid for three and a half years."

A look of compassion overtook Jet's tanned face. "Isn't that long enough to be afraid, Liz? You can't live like that."

Yes, I could. I had been living like that. If Jet meant always being afraid was a terrible way to live, I agreed, but saw no way out for myself.

Jet asked me if Vic or Jaku dated anyone at the station.

"Jaku didn't," I said. "Vic and I double-dated once, with Tony and Annie."

Randy turned to Jet. "Tony is the firefighter who showed up at the scene with Liz," he explained, then looked at me. "Have you ever been over to Vic's apartment?"

"Twice. Once when we met there for our date—Vic and I, Tony and Annie—and once when I brought him a potted plant after he had a minor surgery."

"You and Vic were just friends, then? Not boyfriend and girlfriend?" Jet asked.

"Just friends."

My mind replayed memories of hoping for more on Vic's and my double date. Of the excitement I'd felt hanging out with him at his place. Thoughts of how unreal Vic's death was overtook me until Jet saying, "Liz?" pulled me back into the present.

I started to shake.

Jet must have noticed because he asked, "Where do you think most accidents in the home occur, Liz?"

"I . . . I . . . don't know."

"In the bathtub. People fall. Do you think they should stop taking showers because they might slip and fall?"

"I guess not."

"Fear is just fear," Jet said. "You can't let it rule your life."

I imagined, being a cop, Jet must know all about fear. But I didn't believe being afraid of falling in the bathroom could be nearly as terrifying as feeling the aftershock of a murder.

"Did you know Christian's in custody?" Jet asked.

At the station, we'd joked about Jaku's mom being overly optimistic, giving her son a name like Christian. "I wasn't sure he still was," I said. "That makes me feel better." My shaking subsided. "We call him Jaku."

Jet grabbed a stool and set it down a few inches from my chair. "Did Jaku and Vic date the same woman?"

"I don't know what they did when they weren't at work. They hung out together but I can't imagine any girl liking both of them, they were so different."

"Do they have girlfriends?" Jet asked.

I shrugged.

"Kind of unusual isn't it, two bachelors with no girlfriends?" Jet raised an eyebrow.

"Vic used to have a girlfriend," I said. "He talked about a hairdresser named Molly. She lived with him for six months. They split up eight months ago, and he didn't mention anyone else since then. As for Jaku, he bragged about all these women he'd supposedly been with but he was probably lying."

"A pellet gun was found at the scene," Jet said. "Do you know if either of them owned a pellet gun?"

I shook my head. "Last December, right after he got passed up for a promotion, Jaku told me he might get a job as a security guard. Maybe he got a pellet gun for his job?"

The detectives looked at each other and then back at me but they didn't say a word. I continued, "He hasn't been at work for six weeks, so maybe he was working somewhere else. For the past month, he kept calling in sick. He had to come back to work this morning with a doctor's excuse or else the chief was going to fire him."

"Do you have any idea what Jaku's been doing these last six weeks?"

I shook my head. "I wish I did."

Jet wiped his forehead with a handkerchief. "It sure is hot in here."

"Sorry." I jumped up and cranked the jalousies open. Immediately, trade winds whipped through the room. "I was heading to a friend's house. I'll call her, tell her I'll be late." I dialed Candy's phone number but got a busy signal.

Suddenly, it was all too much—the detectives staring at me, Vic dead, Jaku in custody for now but for all I knew he might be released tomorrow. I started shaking and couldn't stop.

"Oh, we caught you as you were leaving," Randy said.

"We'll go," Jet said.

I escorted them to the front door. Randy thanked me for my help and Jet handed me his card. "The number for Homicide is on the back," Jet said. "Call us if you think of anything else you want to tell us."

At that moment I couldn't think of a single thing.

Friday, February 15, the Day after Vic

I barely made it to work in time for eight o'clock roll call, too late to talk to the off-going firemen on Vic's shift. Sadness filled me at the thought I should stop thinking of A-shift as Vic's shift since he was never coming back.

The Hawai'ian sky seemed to echo my grief, for raindrops pinged on the station's roof and blew against the picture windows. Shedding tears for Vic. Why wasn't I shedding tears as well? Why did I feel so numb? Horror filled me as I reflected on the awful aberration of Vic's life being snuffed out, not by a fire fought in the line of duty, but by a gun in the hand of a man he considered a friend.

My thoughts circled in an endless, anxious loop as I worried Jaku would make bail. Had Jaku planned to come gunning for the chief because he passed him up for a promotion? Was the argument about that?

I glanced through the picture window facing the airfield trucks at the rapid response Ramp 7 pickup, sandwiched between the chief's sparkling pickup and a large, shining airfield truck. Ramp 7 was splattered with mud across its red chassis and silver wheel rims.

The sight irritated me. Vic never would have allowed anything less than spotless for his speedy steed. If Vic were still alive, the Ramp 7 driver on B-shift, not wanting to incur Vic's anger, would have polished the truck before roll call until it shone like a waxed red apple.

"Liz." Deputy Chief Bob's voice startled me out of my reverie.

"Yes?"

"Some detectives phoned." Bob leaned against the alarm room door. "They said they would drive out if anybody was willing to talk to them about Vic and Jaku. Off the record, if they like. I told them I would."

Jaku had described Bob as "the chief's boy" and a "bolo head porky," meaning balding and fat. For his part, Bob had thought of Jaku as an all-talk-no-walk braggart. I wondered what he thought of Jaku now.

I swiveled in my secretarial chair to face Bob. "As long as it's off the record, I'll talk to them."

He smiled and said he was proud of me for coming forward. He asked me to call everyone to the training room while he phoned the detectives back.

The firemen welcomed a break from the brooms, mops and sponges of station cleanup, but declined to talk to the cops. They said they didn't work on A-shift with Vic and Jaku, didn't know the two men well, and therefore had nothing to say. Their response disappointed me because some of them had worked on A-shift for years.

"When I told the detectives who they'd be speaking to, they said, 'Oh, yes, we know Liz'," Bob said. "They'll come back tomorrow, too, when A-shift is on duty."

"Good." Hopefully the guys who'd worked with Vic would talk to Jet and Randy.

By the time the detectives arrived, the rain had stopped and a bright rainbow spanned the sky from Whaler's runway to the craggy Koolau Mountains in the north. They used the chief's office as their interview room and talked with Bob first.

I waited beside the closed door, looking through a window at tall coconut palm trees and scarlet bougainvillea shrubs, glistening with raindrops in front of the station. When the door opened, I heard Bob's parting words, "The chief has a heart of gold. Jaku slapping him was grounds for dismissal, but the chief knew Jaku had a son to support and gave him another chance."

Jaku supporting a son? News to me. Probably just another one of his lies.

"Hello, Liz." Jet ushered me into the office, motioned me to sit in the chief's executive chair. The detectives looked sharp in their black slacks and aloha shirts. I felt underdressed in my blue jeans and red T-shirt.

They faced me in straight-backed chairs across the chief's large oak desk.

"Chief Green must be a good-hearted man," Jet remarked.

"Bob thinks so." I shrugged. "Most of us think the chief's afraid of Jaku."

Randy raised an eyebrow. "Why?"

"Because he didn't fire Jaku after Jaku slapped him."

A year and a half earlier, Jaku had acted out the episode for me in the alarm room. Several weeks after I talked with the detectives, a fireman told me what really happened. The chief had pointed his finger at Jaku and scolded him for some wrong doing. Jaku pushed his finger down but then realized what he'd done. "I got a son to support," Jaku pleaded. "I'm sorry, eh?" The chief gave Jaku a second chance but warned him he would be fired if he were insubordinate again.

Jet frowned. "Why do you think the chief was afraid of Jaku?"

"Because Jaku's a . . ." I searched for the right word, "a criminal. He committed lots of crimes, all of them behind someone's back."

"Like what?" Jet watched me intently.

"Like setting his car on fire in the cane fields when he couldn't make the payments, so he could collect from the insurance company. Like, with the help of what he said were his Mafia connections, ripping off the station's two-thousand-dollar VCR and TV and selling them at the swap meet. Like ripping off the firemen's wallets and lockers until they got wise and locked everything up when Jaku was working."

I breathed deeply, but my heart still raced. "Then there was an incident with Ed Jones, a firefighter who used to work here." I paused, remembering. The Ed Jones story had scared me most of all.

"Can you tell us about the incident?" Jet prompted.

"Ed disliked Jaku but knew better than to confront him. Soon after Ed left Whaler, he turned Jaku in to the Security Police for smoking pot in the bunkrooms. Fortunately for Jaku, a policeman friend of his tipped him off. Jaku managed to dump his stash before the SPs came with the dogs to sniff the place out. They found nothing."

"A few weeks later, Jaku sent some of his thug friends over to Ed's house. Ed wasn't there but his mother and brother were. The thugs beat them up so badly they ended up in the Intensive Care Unit at the hospital."

* * *

I'd been Jaku's captive audience in the alarm room when he acted out the Ed Jones story.

"Hey, the bugger never should have messed with me, no joke."

Jaku threw his hands in the air, wriggled his eyebrows, and paced the floor. "Us guys used to drink plenty beers in the bunkrooms, Ed too, so how come he never told his asshole cop buddies about him being a bunkroom boozer? He never wanted to point the finger at himself, is why, the f . . . ing hypocrite." Jaku curled his hand into a pretend gun and acted like he was shooting an imaginary Ed. "No way is the big prick going to get away with turning my ass in without getting his own ass kicked. No f . . . ing way."

The familiar taste of fear coated my tongue. Again, I wished I dared tell Jaku to get out.

* * *

Jet looked at Randy and then at me. "All of these things really happened?"

"Yes."

"Did Jaku tell you about all of them?"

"Only a few of them," I said. "The firemen told me the rest."

"Why do you think Jaku told you about a few of these things?" Randy asked.

"Because he knew I'd listen. He didn't know I was afraid not to. But Jaku liked to brag to almost everybody, not just me. I think most of the guys knew better than to ignore him or make him mad because he would have slashed their tires or worse."

In an incredulous tone of voice, Jet asked, "Why didn't you tell the chief about these things?" He immediately answered his own question. "You were scared, weren't you?"

"Yes. I figured the chief was scared, too, because he let Jaku get away with slapping him. Jaku gets even with people who confront him, like he did with Ed Jones."

Randy asked, "Did Jaku ever say anything to you against any particular race?

"He called Japanese Americans . . ." I paused. Jet signaled me to go on. ". . . slant-eyed Buddha Heads, and said they all stick together."

"Did he ever say anything against haoles?" Jet asked.

I nodded. "I overheard him saying something about 'f . . . ing haoles' a couple of times when he didn't know I was listening."

Jet must have sized me up as a good witness because he pulled a tape recorder from his briefcase. "We'd like you to make a statement."

My heartbeat sped up. "You said we could talk to you off the record."

"Off the record won't help us with the judge, Liz. If we tell him what you said, he'll ask, 'Where's her statement?'"

Fear wrenched up the volume of my voice. "Can you guarantee me protection 24 hours a day?"

"No," Jet said softly.

"But Jaku will send his thugs after me if I testify against him in court!" *He tricked me. He said we could talk to him off the record.*

"Jet, she lives alone," Randy said.

"So what?" Jet captured me in the steady gaze of his executioner eyes. "What if you had a family? Would you tell the truth then? You said Vic was your friend. What if he was your brother? Would you tell the truth about Jaku if Vic was your brother?"

His words stabbed me and I cringed.

"So," Jet said, "you have a conscience."

"I felt like . . . in many ways . . . he was my brother," I whispered.

"Won't you tell the truth for your brother?"

Blood rushed out of my head. I felt faint, squeezed between fear of Jaku and love for Vic. In the face of all the possibilities circling through my head of how Jaku would hurt me if I testified against him, I couldn't think clearly. The moral obligation, to tell the truth no matter what Jaku did to me, also tormented me and made me feel even more scattered and stressed out.

The only way I could think of to give myself some space was to say, "I only worked with their shift eight hours a day, two or three times a week. Why don't you question the guys on A-shift who worked with them 24 hours a day, three or four shifts a week? Jaku told them a lot more than he told me."

"We intend to. But what about you? Are you going to make a statement?"

Jet's hard gaze unnerved me. *He doesn't understand Jaku's buddies will torture me or worse if I testify against him.* Stalling for time, I said, "I'll think about it."

Jet frowned. He shoved the tape recorder back into his briefcase. "Okay," he said, "You think about it."

I escorted them to the front door. As long as it didn't necessitate me placing my head on Jaku's chopping block, I wanted to give them some piece of information to help put him behind bars. "Jaku had a murder fantasy," I blurted out. "He was always threatening to blow someone away. He was like an explosion about to happen."

Jet and Randy exchanged glances. "We know," Randy said quietly.

* * *

After the detectives left, I stared through the alarm room's picture window at the fire trucks, red sentinels facing the taxiway, lined up to rescue an airplane in distress. But who would rescue me?

Anxious thoughts circled through my head: *What should I do? Can the cops force me to make a statement about what I told them? Will I have to testify? How can I protect myself from Jaku? Has he told his thugs where I lived? Should I stay with friends?*

I decided to ask my father. Although my self-esteem had suffered under his iron rule, things were better between us now, with me out from under his roof. I still chaffed against the habit of command sitting squarely on his retired Air Force Brigadier General shoulders, but I also appreciated his rock-solidness when I needed level-headed advice.

That evening, cool trade winds gusted through the open windows of my living room, billowing the white curtains and playing a monotone tune on my bamboo wind chimes. I left the living room lamps off in case someone was watching my apartment with binoculars, but light from the naked lightbulb dangling from the ceiling of the outside walkway cast sufficient light through my window slats to see the numbers on the phone.

I called my parents and filled them in.

"I don't care what the cops told you, I don't want you to make a statement," my father insisted.

"No, dear, you shouldn't," Mom echoed, her voice camouflaged by static on their portable phone.

For once, the three of us agreed. "I'm scared. I think Jaku was coming to work to murder some supervisors," I said, my face heating up despite the breeze cooling my cheeks. "Maybe some firemen, too, because he thought they'd crossed him."

"What makes you think so?" Dad asked.

"Jaku was cocksure he'd be promoted to captain last December, but the chief gave the job to someone else." I tried to keep my voice steady. "The next day, Jaku went on annual leave for two weeks. After two weeks, he called in sick for a whole month. Yesterday was the day he had to come back to work with a doctor's excuse or be fired."

"How does Vic play into all of this?" Dad's slow, quiet voice calmed me.

Tony and I had talked about this. "We're guessing Jaku wanted Vic to give him a ride because his Toyota wouldn't start," I said. "At least, the hood was up. Jaku probably showed Vic his .357 Magnum and told him he was going to blow some shirts away, and Vic said, 'No you're not!' They argued and Jaku probably plugged him with the bullets he meant for us and—"

"Now, wait a minute, honey. Calm down."

"Okay," I whispered.

"You're jumping to a whole lot of unfounded conclusions," Dad continued. "There are a few things I want to ask you. Okay?"

"Okay," I repeated.

"Did you ever go out with this Jaku character?"

"No way!"

"Did you ever do anything to make him mad at you?"

"No. I worked hard not to upset him because I was afraid of him."

"Did you ever actually see him commit any crimes?"

"No. He just told me about the things he did."

"Good." Dad sounded relieved. "Everything you've told me is hearsay evidence and inadmissible as evidence in court."

I figured my father should know, and felt better.

"A man will tell a girl a lot of things if he wants to impress her," Dad added.

"True," I said, "but the police said they'll need my statement to show the judge or else what I told them won't be admissible in court."

"Oh, horse feathers!" I smiled at my father's favorite expression. "Don't give them one. The cops are lying to you. It wouldn't be admissible in court anyway. All the things you've told me about are hearsay. Take my advice. Don't tell the cops a thing."

"I've already told them a lot, off the record."

"Well, that's okay, Liz," my father said. "You've done your duty as a citizen. But don't sign your name to anything. Now listen to your dad. I've sat on a lot of courts-martial, and put more God-damned criminals behind bars than you can shake a stick at. I know how the courts operate. Don't make a statement."

"Okay, I won't." I breathed deeply, grateful I didn't have to. "I'm afraid of what Jaku's thug friends would do to me if I testified against him."

"I can certainly see why you'd feel apprehensive, dear," my mom said softly. "And you wouldn't want to say anything to make him mad at you, anything you'd have to repeat in court."

"I sure wouldn't, Mom."

I thanked them for their sound advice. After I hung up the phone, loneliness washed over me in my too-quiet apartment. I thought about Vic, how humorous and high energy he'd been, and how my world collapsed after he left it. Would I ever find a path through the darkness I had fallen into without Vic's smile to light my way?

Chapter 5

Saturday, February 16, the Second Day after Vic

After dinner, Assistant Chief Maxwell asked me to page Mike, Lino, and Emilio to the chief's office, where the detectives awaited them. A few minutes later, on my way to a bathroom break, I spotted Jet and Randy, and waved.

"We've been talking to Jaku," Jet said. "Have you been receiving obscene phone calls?"

His question stopped me. I didn't want to talk about the phone call, but there was no escaping Jet's perceptive eyes. I tried to stall, "You mean, in the station?"

Jet looked startled. "Have you EVER received any obscene phone calls?" Frowning, he pointed at a chair in the chief's office. "Come here and sit down."

Reluctantly, I obeyed. "One," I admitted, "at my apartment."

"When was this?" Jet watched me like a cat watches a mouse.

"About four months ago, shortly after midnight."

* * *

The previous October, moments after I arrived home from work, a week after Jaku was booted out of the alarm room, my phone rang. The caller spoke in a stage whisper, his voice rhythmic, "Oh, I want to kiss you all over, I want to smell your panties, I want to . . ." I dropped the receiver but heard him moan, "Oh, baby, I'm coming right now."

His raspy voice, fevered and insistent, etched itself into my memory. I'd wanted to see if I could recognize the voice, but now I regretted not hanging up immediately, and unplugged the phone. I wondered if the caller knew L. Hartz, as I'm listed in the phone book, was a woman, or if he just got lucky.

The following evening at work, Vic and five other firemen lounged on chairs in the office adjacent to the alarm room, and talked story with me. When I told them I had received an obscene phone call the night before, Vic asked, "Was it Jaku?"

"No. I didn't recognize the voice. But the caller phoned right after I got home, as if he knew my schedule."

"You live alone, yeah, Liz?" one of the firemen asked.

My heart beat faster. How did he know? "Not any more. Billy's back," I lied.

"Good thing," he said. "You heard about the Makiki rapist, yeah?"

"Yes." I worried about the rapist. He stalked my neighborhood and only attacked women who lived alone.

* * *

"Did you recognize the voice?" Jet asked.

I shook my head. "It wasn't Jaku."

The detectives looked at each other, and then back at me. A glance over my shoulder revealed Emilio leaning against the secretary's desk, looking like he would rather be anywhere else. "Do you want to talk to Emilio now?" I asked.

Jet smiled. "Yes. We'll talk to you later."

I felt smug knowing he wouldn't.

Lino told me later he and Emilio and Mike would be subpoenaed to testify Jaku showed them his loaded gun when he brought it to the station. Lino had been a friend of Vic's, and I figured that was why he had volunteered this information.

Still, finding out that the firemen had not told the chief about the gun stunned me. Maybe Lino, like most of the firemen, either believed

Jaku was just a bunch of hot air or else was as afraid of him as I was. The only fireman I knew with certainty had not been afraid of Jaku was Vic. But then again, Vic was dead.

Sunday, February 17, the Third Day after Vic

I woke up sweating on that windless, humid Sunday morning, overwhelmed by a feeling of loss. My belly cramped and my chest ached. I felt like a mirror struck by a fist, with grief pouring in to fill the cracks.

I'd been anesthetized since the murder, a sleepwalker propelled by adrenaline, just going through the motions of living. Now a strong impression of Vic slapping his chest, amazed and delighted to discover he still existed, came over me.

I saw Vic so clearly in my mind's eye I could almost touch him. He crossed his muscular arms across his chest, looked at me with those alive eyes of his, shook his head at my foolishness, and dropped one side of his mouth in mock reproach, the way he did when he teased me. As waves of grief rolled through me I could almost hear him say, "Can't you see? I'm right here, Snake."

Could he really be present in spirit? I thought about Jesus rising from the tomb on the third day, and wondered if all spirits resurrected after three days.

A jarring sensation, like an internal earthquake, shook my chest and head four times in rapid succession, wham, wham, wham, wham! It was eerie, and I trembled.

Part of me wondered if I'd lost it. Another part thought I might be experiencing a connection with Vic. I'd read in a metaphysical book that emotional ties facilitate contact between the so-called dead and the living. Maybe my love and grief were drawing Vic's spirit to me.

"Vic." I don't know why I whispered. "I think you're here." My head tingled the way it does when I experience something psychic in nature.

Hours later, my sorrow receded. I lay like a rag doll on my damp mattress, completely spent, ice cubes wrapped in napkins pressed against my sore eyes. A feeling of peace enveloped me. I fell asleep, the soggy napkins still soothing my eyes.

I didn't wake up until three o'clock in the afternoon, and had to rush to make it to work by four. In the evening, when Deputy Chief Bob asked me if I was okay, tears stung my bloodshot eyes. I blinked them away, swallowed hard, and shook my head.

He pressed a warm hand to my shoulder, said, "I'm right next door if you want to talk," and closed the alarm room door behind him.

When darkness fell, I dimmed the lights so no one could see me crying through the one-way glass. I consoled myself with knowing midnight was mere hours away and I would have the next two days off.

Monday, February 18, through Monday, February 25

The following morning, loud knocking on my front door dashed my hopes of sleeping in. I pulled on a T-shirt and jeans, squinted through the slats of my jalousie window, and spotted Tony. Unlocking the door, I motioned him in. "What's up?" I yawned.

He glanced at his wristwatch. "I called the prosecutor's office. The preliminary hearing starts at District Court in 30 minutes. Want to go?"

I immediately felt alert. "Yes! Thanks for staying on top of things."

"I thought you'd want to go." Tony playfully cocked his head, the way he did when he wanted to make me smile. "You and Vic were tight. Him and me, too, and Annie. He'd want us to be there."

"You are true blue," I said, a catch in my voice.

He drove me in his green Ford pickup through bumper-to-bumper traffic. I ran a brush through my hair and asked, "Is Annie working?"

"Yes, but she's going to take leave. She'll meet us there. Her brother Grip will meet us at court."

"Grip?" Had I heard him right? "Like in, 'Get a Grip?'"

Tony laughed. "Real name's Ben. He used to wrestle professionally and was known for his iron grip, hence the nickname. Anyway, he spoke on the phone to Jaku this morning, but he didn't say what about."

"How does he know Jaku?" I blinked in the glaring sunlight.

"I took him with me to a poker game at Jaku's place once, when Jaku and I were still sociable," Tony said. "I think he went back on his own a few times."

District Court was in an ancient wooden building in an old section of downtown Honolulu. Tony drove around for fifteen minutes before he could find parking. We ran up three steep flights of stairs to the courtroom because the elevator was broken, and spotted Chief Green sitting on a bench in the hallway. He said the hearing had begun about ten minutes earlier. Tony pushed the heavy Koa-wood door open, and we hurried inside.

Thirteen local people sat on benches to the left of the doorway. We slid onto a bench on the right. "Those folks are Jaku's mom and dad, his three sisters, their husbands and kids, and a couple of cousins," Tony said. "I met them at a party at Jaku's place a couple of months ago."

Jaku sat at a large desk at the front of the courtroom beside a short, balding, Japanese-American man, both of them wearing suits. Ironically, Jaku's lawyer was a member of the race he called Buddha heads. Jaku's springy mat of hair was clipped so short he appeared to be wearing a black skullcap.

Jet was on the stand, saying, "And one more piece of evidence indicative of foul play ..."

Jaku's lawyer shot to his feet. "Objection."

"Yes, Mr. Nozawa?" said the judge.

"I move the detective's judgments be stricken from the record on the grounds he does not qualify as an expert witness."

"I've been in Homicide for eleven years." Jet frowned. "I've seen hundreds of homicides." His gray eyes took in the spectators as he waited for the judge's decision.

"This is an important point," Tony whispered. "If the detective's opinions are not permitted, the State will have a weaker case."

"The court will allow Detective Yamasato's observations," the judge said. "Objection overruled. Continue, Detective."

"One more piece of evidence indicative of foul play," Jet repeated. "Perfect grip on the gun with the right hand. Very unusual. Most of the time, the gun falls out of the hand when a person is shot in a standing-up position."

A tall, olive-skinned man sporting a handlebar mustache squeezed past my knees and sat between Tony and me. He and Tony whispered back and forth for a few minutes. Then Tony pointed at me.

The man twisted to face me. "You're Liz?"

I nodded.

He smiled and extended his hand, "I'm Annie's brother, Grip."

We shook hands. He added, "Have you been receiving obscene phone calls?"

"One, about four months ago. Why?"

Grip grimaced. "Lying bastard—excuse me, Liz. When I talked to Jaku, he ranted for half an hour about how Vic was making obscene phone calls to you, and how he was threatening to report Vic to the chief for harassing you, and that's what the argument was about."

I frowned. "No way could the caller have been Vic. He had a local accent."

Grip shrugged. "I don't know Jaku well. I just played poker and drank beer with him and some other firemen a couple of times. Seems like a flipped-out dude."

Ernesto, a short Filipino man who lived in the apartment above Jaku, took the stand. He testified he had heard a loud argument, followed by five or six rapid shots, and then silence. He ran down the stairs leading into the garage and saw Vic lying on the concrete floor face up, his head in a pool of blood.

"Where was Vic's right hand?" the prosecuting attorney asked.

"I never notice." Ernesto spoke in a thick pidgin accent. Sweat beaded on his forehead. "I was tripping on the blood around his head, freaking out, looking at all the blood."

The next three witnesses were firefighters from Whaler. Lino took the stand first, followed by Emilio and then Mike. All three testified they had seen Jaku bring a loaded .357 Magnum to the fire station. They identified the weapon exhibited in the courtroom as looking like the same weapon.

Grip whispered something to Tony, squeezed past our knees, and walked out. "Grip said there's enough evidence to hold a trial, no doubt about it," Tony said. "If it was an obvious case of self-defense, as Jaku claimed, there'd be no need."

The judge called a recess. Everyone filed into the hallway. Annie, her high heels clicking loudly across the tile floor, joined us. Tony filled her in on what had transpired. After hearing about Vic's right hand found gripping a gun, she said, "Liz, wasn't Vic a leftie?"

I searched my memory. "No. When I read his palm, I read the right one because it was his experience hand."

"You read palms? What about the left one?" Annie asked.

"It shows the soul's plan for this lifetime. But the experience hand shows what a person does with the plan. In Vic's case, the two hands were almost identical."

"Interesting." Tony cradled one of Annie's dimpled, manicured hands between his bony ones and asked her, "Speaking of hands, did I tell you Liz read mine?"

"Yes," she smiled. "She said you're going to marry me."

I had only told Tony he would marry by the time he was thirty-five or so, but I let it slide. "I only know the main lines so I'm not a full-fledged palmist," I explained. "But it's fun to read palms, except for—oh my god."

"What?" Tony asked.

"I just thought about reading Jaku's palm last November." I felt faint. "It was a total freak out."

"Why?"

Should I tell him? If I did, he'd probably think I was a nut case. Well, too late to stop now. "Because he has murderer's thumbs." If only I'd thought to warn Vic.

"Really?" Annie's eyes widened. "What do they look like?"

"They're shaped like little cave man clubs." I drew a picture in the air with my index fingers. "They don't necessarily mean the person will murder, but they do indicate a violent temper and a tendency, when angered, to reach for the closest weapon."

"Did you tell Jaku about it?" Annie asked.

"Are you kidding? I tried to warn him about his temper, though. But he blew it off. It wasn't what he wanted to hear."

* * *

On a slow, muggy night in the alarm room, I told Vic I'd taken a weekend palmistry class nine years earlier and could read a few lines and mounds.

"Yeah?" Vic raised an eyebrow as he pulled his chair close to mine. He laid his large, wide paw on the white console next to my slim, long-fingered hand. He had the flat, open palm of a man who didn't hide inside of himself, unlike mine with its large cavity in the center. I held his warm hand and said, "Well, you're not in a rut. See, there are no rut lines on your fingers," and I showed him my fingers so he could see what rut lines looked like.

"You have a long lifeline, no breaks, no serious illnesses," I added. "Oh, wow. Look at your large Mound of Venus." I ran a red fingernail across the mound beneath Vic's thumb. Even though a large mound merely indicates a passionate nature which can manifest in any number of ways, I smiled and said, "It means you're a great lover."

A skeptical expression crossed Vic's tanned face. "Yeah, right," he said, so I figured he knew I was flirting. But maybe he didn't because he must have talked about it to Jaku, who hurried into the alarm room soon after Vic left, waved his hands in my face, and demanded, "Am I a better lover than Vic, or what?"

I gingerly held Jaku's hand. "Let's see." Even though his mound of Venus was flat, I told him, "Like Mohammad Ali, you are the greatest." He smiled, nodding, and wriggled his eyebrows at me. Then I saw his murderer's thumbs.

"Remember to watch your temper," I whispered.

He frowned. "I'm a better lover than Vic, yeah?"

* * *

I told Tony, "Jaku's thumbs look exactly like the murderer's thumbs in my palmistry book."

"I wouldn't mention it to the detectives," Tony said. "They're going to want 'the facts, ma'am, just the facts.'"

"I know what you mean." I kind of liked the idea of telling the detectives. Maybe they would think I was airy fairy and wouldn't want me to testify.

"I'm going to talk to Jaku's mom for a minute," Annie said. Tony and I watched, stunned, as she walked toward the drinking fountain where Jaku's family gathered together.

"Why would she talk to Jaku's family?" I asked.

Tony shook his head and frowned. "Beats the hell out of me."

Glancing after Annie, I spotted Jet leaning against the hallway wall, arms crossed, scrutinizing Jaku's family. I asked Tony, "Do you know when Vic's family will arrive?"

"No," he said, his voice clipped.

"I think I'll ask Jet."

Tony nodded. "I'll wait here for Annie."

I walked toward Jet. A short local man left Jaku's family group and headed my way. He stopped about three feet away from Jet and me, raised his upper lip in a sneer, and glared at us.

Jet ignored the man and raised an eyebrow at me.

"There's something I'd like to ask you," I began, before pausing, wondering why the stranger didn't back off and if I should talk to Jet in his presence.

"Yes?" Jet continued to ignore the man.

Taking my cue from him, I asked, "Is Vic's family arriving soon?"

"In a few days." He looked at me appraisingly. "You're not still scared, are you?"

I frowned, shook my head, and turned away, not realizing until later my head shake was a lie because I was terrified of what Jaku would do to me if I testified against him. Tony later told me the short local man was the "bad-ass cousin" who, Jaku claimed, helped him burglarize expensive homes on the windward side.

Tony and Annie stood opposite the courtroom door, arguing. I joined them as Annie announced angrily, "I'm going back to the office." She marched away.

"What's wrong?" I asked Tony.

He jammed his hands in his pockets. "I got mad at her for talking to Jaku's mom. She said she didn't want it to look like it's the haoles against the locals, you know. She told Mrs. Cardoza she felt sorry for her and her family in this time of trouble."

I hadn't considered Jaku's parents. "What did Mrs. Cardoza say?"

"She's angry at her husband because he doesn't want to put up their house to raise the bail for Jaku, and they're fighting about it." Tony shrugged. "I told Annie I couldn't care less about Jaku's family, and she got mad and left."

"I'm with you. I'd say Vic and his family are the victims here." I glanced at the piece of paper taped inside the courtroom door. "Two more to testify, the other detective and Chief Green."

We agreed we had probably heard everything we needed to hear.

On the way home, I told Tony I'd reconsidered. "Annie has a point. Jaku's family isn't to blame for Jaku's actions."

Tony said he was thinking the same thing and would give Annie a call.

Later in the afternoon, the chief phoned and told me Jaku's bail had been set at fifty thousand dollars.

"Why would they let a murderer out on any amount of bail?" I asked.

"Ah, but our justice system assumes a man is innocent until proven guilty," he answered. "I think we can take heart. Fifty grand is unusually high for a murder case. It's normally twenty thousand."

The next day, Tuesday, February 19, was my first day off since Vic's death. Normally, I slept in on days off, but anger at Jaku claiming Vic made obscene calls to me kept me awake. I decided that what my father had said about hearsay evidence didn't apply to the obscene phone call because it actually happened to me. Jet wanted a statement, so I would give him one, get him off my back, and show Jaku up as a liar at the same time.

I dialed Homicide. Randy answered and told me Jet wasn't there. I asked Randy if I could talk to him instead, and make a statement.

"Yes, you can come down in 15 minutes," Randy sounded pleased. With a little luck, I would be gone before Jet returned.

I sat on a hard wooden bench in the police station's dirty hallway while the receptionist phoned Randy to tell him I was there. A few minutes later, he escorted me to a small room furnished only with a scarred wooden table and two metal folding chairs.

"Care for a cup of coffee?" he said.

I nodded. The coffee tasted bitter but its warmth was welcome in the icy room. "I'd like to make a statement about the obscene phone call," I said.

A look of disbelief followed by disappointment flitted across Randy's face. "Why?"

"I heard Jaku was telling lies about me getting obscene phone calls from Vic, and I want to set the record straight. And because I now think the obscene caller was Jaku."

"Why?" Randy repeated.

"Because the caller spoke with a local accent, and he must have known my work schedule because he phoned as soon as I returned home after the swing shift. And I suspect he knew L. Hartz, as I'm listed in the phone book, was a woman."

Randy raised an eyebrow. "If you make a statement about this, you'll have to tell us what the caller said."

"I'll have to repeat what I say? It's embarrassing."

"The judge will ask you to repeat it if you're called upon to testify."

Surely I wouldn't have to testify about something as insignificant as an obscene phone call at a murder trial.

He added, "You can either write it down or speak into a tape recorder."

I opted to write it down. Randy read my statement, rubbed his chin, and said, "Jaku could easily have disguised his voice. Why did Vic ask, 'Was it Jaku?'"

"Because Jaku's a pervert, and everybody knows it."

Randy escorted me to the station's front door. He thanked me for making a statement but he didn't look happy about it. His reaction made me uneasy, but I also felt relieved.

Back at my apartment, a note on my door read, "Vic's sisters and their husbands arrived in Honolulu today. They'll be at Vic's place. The funeral's set for Friday. Tony."

You're the best, Tony. Maybe I could do something for Vic's family. I decided to drive to his place after my midnight shift.

On the following morning, tired from zero sleep, I trudged sadly up three flights of stairs to apartment 409. Both times I had been inside, everything was clean and neat, not a dish or free weight out of place. But now phonograph records, clothes, barbells, and more were strewn across carpet, kitchen counters, and couch. Two men, one tall and thin, the other short and stout, stood in the tiny living room. A woman with curly brown hair sat on the carpet, crying and sorting through dishes.

Another woman with wavy black hair stared at me through the open door. She smiled and said, "Hello."

"Hello." A lump formed in my throat.

"Were you a friend of Vic's?"

I nodded. "I'm just shattered by what happened and . . . and . . ." I started crying.

The woman cried, too. Then she wiped her eyes, held my shoulders, and said, "It's all right. Vic's with God now."

I sniffled, "True."

The tall man handed us tissues and stared at me through wire-rimmed glasses. "Would you like to sit down?"

"Yes. Thanks."

He pulled out the kitchen chair I'd sat in when Vic whipped me up a hamburger-helper meal. My eyes got misty at the thought, *Vic won't do that or anything else ever again. Our good times are all gone.*

"I'm Mike Summers," the man said. He gestured toward the black-haired woman. "And this is my wife Lola, Vic's sister." Mike pointed at the other woman, who continued to cry. "Vic's other sister Betty."

"I'm so sorry, Betty and Lola and Mike—," my voice broke.

Mike pointed at the short man. "This is Betty's husband, Joe."

"And Joe. I'm Liz, I worked with Vic, and we were friends, and if there's anything I can do, anything at all, I am happy to help," I said in one long breath. "These are cramped quarters for four people. I just live a few blocks away. Two of you are welcome to stay with me."

Lola's smile was dimpled like Vic's. She said she appreciated the kind offer but Chief Green had already arranged for accommodations for Betty and Joe at a hotel. She and Mike were staying here so they could more easily sort through Vic's belongings and decide what to ship home and what to give to his friends.

"I can contact Vic's friends for you when you're ready," I offered.

"Thanks. That would help," Lola said.

At least I could do something. "Will your parents be coming?"

She shook her head. "Mom's afraid to fly, and dad just doesn't have the heart."

"I'm sorry." I wondered what could possibly keep a father from his son's funeral.

As if she could read my mind, Lola added, "Dad was on the USS Arizona when Pearl Harbor was bombed. He saw so many of his friends buried at Punchbowl Memorial Park, and couldn't bear to go there again for the funeral of his only son."

"I sympathize with how your father must feel." Not knowing what else to say, I wrote down my phone number and repeated, "Please call if you need anything."

She tried to smile. "I feel better knowing Vic had a friend who cared so much about him. Thanks for coming over. Will you be coming to the funeral tomorrow?"

"Oh, yes." I wanted to say something comforting but the only words I could come up with were, "All of us at the fire department are so sorry this happened. So very sorry."

Lola's eyes flooded with tears. "Goodbye," Mike said.

* * *

At the memorial home the next day, I felt Vic's presence, alive and aware, taking it all in. Still, it was hard to look in the casket and see his face heavy with makeup, looking smaller than I remembered with the life blasted out of him. His head wound was skillfully camouflaged but, to my eye, the patch job was obvious. "Do you see your friends, and coworkers, and family?" I whispered. "We all love you." I joined the others in paying tearful respects to Vic's family.

When the funeral procession assembled, I cried as the pall bearers lifted the casket into Vic's spotless red Ramp 7 truck. Wreathed with garland upon garland of flowers, it led the cavalcade, followed by a red pumper truck, then the individual cars, each with a small black flag stuck on its hood.

The procession wound up the mountain to Punchbowl Cemetery. Slowly we assembled and stood behind the chairs where Vic's family sat, the women in black dresses, the men in black suits, a black mood gripping me as I wondered, *Why, Lord? Why Vic?* When everyone was huddled around the casket, a group of marines marched smartly into place and fired off the twenty-one-gun salute reserved for those who had served in the military.

The minister read a poem Vic's parents had sent about a loving son torn away from the earth in the prime of his life and propelled straight into the arms of God. When he read the words, "Through the quickening years we will love you, son," a tingling sensation wriggled up my spine and neck. At the same moment, a wind whisked briskly beneath the flag the four pall bearers held over the casket, causing it to balloon up, sail-like, almost snatching the flag out of the surprised men's hands.

Oh, Vic, you still love to play. I wiped my eyes with a tissue. *I miss you so.*

***

Two days later, on Saturday day shift, I was typing up the manning sheet when Jim, a quiet, hardworking fireman, plopped down in the chair behind the back desk. "A good buddy of mine who lives in the apartment above Vic heard him arguing the night before he was shot," Jim said. "He figures Vic was on the phone because he only heard Vic's voice."

"Did he hear what Vic was saying?" I asked.

"No," Jim said, "but since he was arguing with someone the night before Jaku shot him, do you suppose the prosecutor could prove premeditated murder?"

"It'd be great if he could. Did your friend tell the detectives about it?" I asked.

"Yeah, when they searched Vic's apartment on the afternoon of his death."

A few hours later, Tony asked if I had heard anything about whether Jaku's bail had been changed or a trial date had been set.

"Not a word," I said. "Should I ask the detectives? I'll bet they know."

"Good idea," Tony said.

On the following Monday, I dialed Homicide and asked to speak with Detective Grabowski or Yamasato. Jet answered the phone, his voice brusque, "Yamasato."

"Hi, Liz here. Do you know if Jaku's bail is still set at fifty thousand? And when the trial will be?"

"Liz," Jet snapped, "what do you think you're doing, making a statement about the obscene phone call?"

I had not expected anger. My heart pounded wildly. I couldn't think clearly as I tried to figure out what stupid or wrong thing I'd done to bring his anger down on me. "I . . . I heard Jaku was saying Vic was making obscene phone calls to me."

"Yeah? So?"

"So I came down and talked about the phone call I received," I whispered, unnerved.

"When are you going to come down and make a statement about what you told us before?" Jet demanded.

"Then I'd have to testify in court?" My legs wobbled and I had to sit.

"Yes! Liz, you must come down. You must! You said Vic was like a brother to you. You must tell the truth for him!"

But I couldn't testify. If I did, Jaku would have me killed. And I couldn't talk about my fears to Jet, who didn't seem to care one whit about my safety. He only cared that the judge be told the truth, and he needed my statement for that.

I had thought I could refuse to make a statement about what I'd told Jet in the chief's office the morning after the murder. After all, it was nothing more than hearsay evidence. But now his anger had me trapped as securely as if I were locked inside a cage. Seeing no way out and not daring to tell The Law to back off, I said, "Okay."

"You must!" Jet insisted. "Think about it for a few days if you like. You can write it down. Or you can tell me when you come down and I'll record your statement. All right, Liz? I expect to see you in a few days."

"Okay," I repeated, thinking, *I already said okay, you bully.*

"All right then!"

I remembered to ask, "How can I find out when Jaku's trial will be? And if his bail's been changed? And if he's still in jail?"

"Call the prosecutor's office." Jet hung up the phone.

The receiver shook in my hand, the shaking spreading until I shook all over. I had no doubt Jaku would send somebody after me if I had to testify against him. How in the world could I protect myself now?

I phoned the prosecutor's office. A woman with a friendly voice said Jaku's trial was now scheduled for June 9, nearly a four month wait because the court was backlogged. No, the bail had not been changed, and yes, Jaku was still in jail.

When I called Tony with the news, he had some for me. During their search of Vic's apartment, the detectives found a loaded .38 lying on top of his futon. The bed was made, indicating Vic placed the gun there after he neatly tucked in the sheets and bedspread around the edges of his futon the morning he was killed.

"I can't believe Vic owned a gun. Was it registered to him?" I said.

"Yes. Vic's family knew he had a .38," Tony said. "They told Jet Vic grew up around guns in the Pennsylvania hills where he was raised, and knew how to use them. But he only fired them during target practice or when he shot poisonous snakes."

"Then it would have been appropriate to use against Jaku," I said. Tony laughed and I asked, "How did you find out?"

He rubbed his hands together. "I haf vays of making people talk."

I smiled, grateful for his humor.

"Actually, the chief told me after the detectives told him. The chief wants me and you and Bob kept in the loop because we're the only ones who voluntarily gave information to the detectives or bothered to show up for the preliminary hearing."

"Good of him."

"Yeah. It's also survival. The more ammunition we can accumulate against Jaku, the better. The scenario the chief and the detectives came up with is Jaku coming to work to shoot him and some of the other supervisors."

"That's what we thought all along," I said. "And Vic tried to stop him."

Tony nodded. "That's the way it looks."

Tuesday, February 26

Although Jaku and Vic affected my dispatching days and nights more than most, they were just two of the forty-three firefighters on A- and B-shifts. Most of the guys were at least cordial, greeting me with, "How's it going, Liz?" Some strolled into the alarm room to talk. A few became friends.

But the bond I shared with my firemen pals was like Elmer's glue compared with the epoxy binding some of them together.

"We're like brothers," a fireman told me. "We trust each other with our lives." I wondered if Vic and Jaku's friendship had been forged during an emergency. But the firemen said no, said Jaku didn't think clearly in a crisis, said he did dangerous things, such as lashing his line onto Bob's air tank inside a burning building, which would have forced Bob to pull off his tank if he got in trouble.

Perhaps Vic and Jaku had connected because they were both hot-shot firemen. Vic's prowess on the fire scene was legendary, but the firemen also considered Jaku a skilled firefighter. "He's fearless in an inferno," one of the guys said, "if it's the kind of big, blazing fire that affords him the limelight." Jaku was in his glory when he smothered roaring flames with foam from the turret atop the huge P-15 airfield truck. "When the world is watching and he can do it from a distance, he never fails to slay the beast," the fireman added.

Sometimes energy flowed between the firefighters and me through the airways, me on the radios, them on the scene where life and death dramas unfolded. Connecting like this provided an incredible rush and I felt privileged to be part of the team. At other times, however, when things were routine and calm, I felt like a member of a dysfunctional family, struggling to cope with personality differences.

Before I started tossing my pee-filled 7-11 coffee cups in the trash, I ran afoul of Gil Flannigan, a talented rescue man and EMT. When I interrupted his volley ball game and sleep to ask for a bathroom break, he angrily called me *Leaky Liz*. After I stopped summoning him so frequently, he became cordial again, although he wasn't one to stop by the alarm room to chat.

After dinner break, I was surprised when Gil walked me back to my cage, as the guys called the alarm room. He blurted out, "You liked Vic, didn't you, Liz?"

I nodded, my eyes instantly teary.

Gil sat behind the back desk. "I'm really sorry for what happened."

I swiveled in my chair to face him. "Thanks." It was all I could say without crying.

"I didn't know Vic and Jaku, being as how they were on the other shift, except to say, 'Hi, how you doing?' to Vic," Gil said. "But I'd heard enough about Jaku to know he was a punk, so I steered clear of him. Did you see the news on TV after he shot Vic?"

I shook my head.

"It showed the police taking Jaku away in the squad car. When he saw the photographer, he made a thumbs-up sign, like he was proud of what he did." Gil's green eyes flashed anger.

"How disgusting, trying to grab the spotlight with Vic lying dead a few feet away."

Gil nodded. "I sat there and cried, Liz, it was such a cold thing to do. Here Jaku had just ripped off the life of his best pal, and he's trying to act like Mr. Cool."

Gil's face blurred as I blinked away tears. "Vic used to joke about Jaku being 'a sick dude.' If only he'd realized just how sick."

"Didn't Jaku like to hang out in the alarm room with you?" Gil asked.

"Yes. I felt trapped."

"It must have been rough, dealing with a psycho in such close quarters."

"Chilling, actually, having to listen to his cruel stories." I shuddered. "What worries me now is Jaku murdering again."

"He's in jail." Gil shrugged. "I've heard rumors about the stories he told, and the crimes he committed. I don't know if any are true. Do you?"

"At least some are. Jaku bragged about committing crimes, but he exaggerated and lied a lot. The things he claimed to have done really happened, though. I've got a theory . . ." My voice shook.

"I'm all ears. Lighten up, girl. Relax."

"Okay." I laughed nervously. "Well, here goes. I figure Jaku killed his own good side when he killed Vic. What remains is dark and deadly."

Gil tried to suppress a smile. "Been reading lots of metaphysical stuff lately?"

"You think I'm a space case? Don't forget, he killed Vic in cold blood." I thought it best not to mention Jaku's murderer's thumbs.

Gil rubbed his chin. "Well, that hasn't been proven. But I imagine it's so."

"He is certainly capable of doing something equally crazy again, what with him looking at serving hard prison time. When some of us have to testify against him, I'm sure he'll try to get even." A sour taste filled my mouth.

Gil's look was part pity and part disdain. "People can't let that punk intimidate them. Jaku will end up behind bars where he belongs. What can he do to us when he's locked up?"

"It's not what he can do—it's what his criminal friends can do," I whispered.

Gil laughed. "Why would they endanger themselves for Jaku when he's facing a murder rap? Do I detect a little paranoia here? Do you have to testify?"

"Maybe." I felt lightheaded, like I might faint. "I'm not sure yet. Yeah, I suppose I'm paranoid. Tomorrow I go down to the police station and give them a statement."

* * *

I slept little on Tuesday night, and worried a lot about what I would say to stop Jet from hassling me further and also make me an unlikely candidate for a witness. I grabbed onto the strategy of focusing Jet's attention on Jaku's sleazy lies and how I'd had him booted out of the alarm room.

I dialed Homicide. "Grabowski," Randy answered.

Perhaps I could avoid talking to Jet by giving my statement to Randy. "I'd like to make a statement. Can I come down?"

"Jet's not here," Randy said.

"Do I have to talk to him?"

"Yes. He'll return soon. Give me your phone number. I'll have him call you back."

Less than five minutes later, the phone rang. "Hello, Liz." Jet's voice was friendly and conversational. "How are you doing? What's up?"

Anxiety made my speech quick and nervous. "I want to come down, right now ... are you busy?"

After a long pause, Jet said, "I'm not busy. You can come down."

"I'll be there in fifteen minutes, I couldn't write it down, I'll just tell you what I know," I blurted out.

Less than ten minutes later, I sat on a hard wooden bench outside the Homicide Division. Could I sidetrack Jet from Jaku's true crime stories? What would happen if I couldn't? My heart pounded faster. Dizzy, I clutched the edge of the bench, stared at the dirty floor, and listened to the air conditioner's drone. What was I doing here after Dad told me not to make a statement?

I looked up to see Jet standing at the entrance to Homicide, staring at me, a compassionate expression on his tanned face. For a moment, he looked more like a kindly gentleman than a stern cop. "Come in, Liz," he said, all business again.

I followed him down a narrow hallway and into a tiny interview room. We sat on hard wooden chairs, facing each other across a card table in the cold, bare cubicle of a room. A tape recorder rested on the table between us.

Jet offered me coffee, but I'd had a taste of Homicide's acidic brew when Randy interviewed me and said, "No thanks."

He poured himself a cup and placed it beside him on the table. "Now, Liz, before we record your statement, let's talk about what we need. I don't want you to tell me what other people told you about Jaku. I need you to tell me the things Jaku told you. Is this clear?"

I nodded and breathed deeply. "Well, he told me he slapped the chief three times and told him, 'If you gonna terminate me, I'm gonna terminate you.' And he told me he stole the station video center equipment and sold it at the swap meet." I paused, hoping this was enough information to appease him.

Jet frowned. "We knew this already. What else—"

"And I had some incidents with Jaku." I looked away. "I don't know if they're important."

Jet leaned forward. "You tell me. I'll tell you if they're important."

I locked eyes with him. "Well . . . the first one happened less than three weeks after I began working at Whaler. The firemen told me Jaku was telling them he had looked through the alarm room window after midnight and . . ." My face flushed. Embarrassment made me mute.

"Go on, Liz." Jet's voice was gentle.

I tried again. "Jaku said he saw me . . ." Again the words stuck in my throat. Finally, I forced them out, "having sex with an Army fire chief on the alarm room floor."

Jet's eyebrows raised high. "Really?"

All I could do was nod.

"Go on."

I forced myself to continue, "I felt humiliated after Jaku told those lies about me, and scared, thinking the firemen would believe him. But, looking back on it now, I see a silver lining. I found out Jaku was a liar and dangerous from the start."

I told Jet about Brian Smith warning me not to confront Jaku. "Brian told me Jaku tried to shoot him, but tripped on a tree root and shot his own toe instead," I relayed. "So I vowed to never do anything to upset Jaku, and started pretending to be his friend so he wouldn't think I was crossing him."

"What other incidents did you have with Jaku?" Jet asked.

"Sergeant Maxwell kicked Jaku out of the alarm room last October because he kept telling me obscene stories. But Jaku didn't know I had complained about him."

"Good that you didn't confront Jaku," Jet said. "You will make a good witness at the trial, Liz. One guy you liked, one guy you didn't. Now I would like you to repeat what you told me, but this time we'll get it on tape, and I'll ask you some questions as we go along."

I repeated my story. It was easier the second time, accompanied by Jet's skillful prompting, but I kept thinking, *what if I have to testify about this stuff?* When he finished taping me, Jet asked, "Does your conscience feel better since you've told the whole truth, Liz?"

"I don't know," I muttered, staring at the floor.

"Now is the time to come forward." Jet's voice radiated confidence. I looked into his gray eyes, admiring him for the sincerity with which he approached his job, but also angry at him for giving me heat. "Now tell me, why were you afraid to confront Jaku?"

"Because I figured, if he'd do those things to other people, he'd do them to me, too."

"Yes!" Jet's voice rang with conviction. "That's not an unreasonable fear."

I felt validated by his words but guilty at my deceit.

Jet told me the slipping-in-the-bathtub story again. "You wouldn't stop taking baths because most home accidents occur in the bath, would you?"

"No."

"Fear is just fear. You can't let it rule your life."

But how do you avoid fear? Jaku really did hurt people and Jet had just said it wasn't unreasonable to think he would hurt me as well. Changing the subject, I said, "Vic said something to me the last time I saw him at work, the day before he was shot. I thought he was just kidding around, teasing me as usual. But then he stretched out his big hands, stuck them in my face, and said, 'Look at the size of these hands'."

I took a deep breath. "Looking back, I think he was trying to tell me he had a conflict with Jaku, and was planning to settle it with his hands. I also think the two of them had been arguing for days, because the firemen tell me Vic was not himself at work for four or five days before he was killed. He almost got in a couple of fights over minor stuff at work. That wasn't like Vic. He was such a mellow, easygoing guy. Something was bothering him."

"What do you think the argument was about?" Jet asked.

"I think Jaku was coming to work on the morning he shot Vic to kill some of the supervisors."

"Yes!" Jet said. "That's what the police think. And Vic blocked his way."

"He was probably trying to talk him out of it. That would be just like Vic."

Jet escorted me to Homicide's front door. "Thank you for coming down."

Embarrassed by his undeserved gratitude, I whispered, "You're welcome."

As I walked away, he called after me, his voice appreciative, "You're helping us."

I turned around and smiled, and quickly turned away. Had I protected myself by holding back? Guilt stabbed me for deliberately omitting what Jaku had said about the crimes he'd committed. Would I have to testify anyway? I shivered and wished I could defeat the fear stalking me like a murderer in the night.

Chapter 6

Thursday, February 28, through Friday, March 8

I FELT LIKE I was trudging through mud rather than climbing three flights of stairs to Vic's former apartment. *Why Vic? Why, God?* My conflicting beliefs, that no man dies before his soul agrees it is time, but also that Vic would never have agreed to be murdered, weighed heavily on me.

A sudden breeze cooled my bare arms and face, sweating from the tropical sun. I thought about how Jaku's murderer's thumbs were a clear sign violent tendencies were his birthright. A less troubled man might have been able to overcome a cruel nature, but Jaku? Was redemption possible for a criminal who saw people either as potential victims or opportunities to thrust himself into the limelight? My conflicting beliefs, that no man dies before his soul agrees it is time but also that Vic would never have agreed to be murdered, weighed heavily on me.

Winded, I sat on the second floor landing and recalled the time I had read Vic's palm. I'd only known how to read the health, life, marriage, and heart lines, a few mounds, and the thumbs. Was there a star or a cross I missed, a sign a more skilled palmist would have seen, indicating Vic's death could be a violent one? Would such a sign mean Vic's death was fate? If so, it was a cruel one, to be dispatching me to his apartment today, on my 34th birthday. I'd hoped to be celebrating the day with him, but instead I would be helping his sister give his belongings away.

I climbed the last two flights of stairs. Through the open front door of number 409, I spotted greasy containers of hamburgers and French fries strewn across the kitchen counters. *I ought to invite them over for a home cooked meal.*

The sight of carefully stacked dishes and pans, clothes, 8-track tapes, and record albums reminded me to mention I had phoned some of Vic's friends and they would be coming over soon. Mike said Lola would be giving away two weight benches, lots of free weights, tapes, albums, and a bicycle, and shipping everything else home.

"How thoughtful of you to give Vic's things to his friends," I said.

"We think Vic would want us to," Mike replied.

"Yes," I said, a catch in my voice.

Lola wrapped a warm arm around my shoulders. "Were you Vic's girlfriend?"

I shook my head and blinked rapidly.

"You seem so broken up about him, we thought you might be."

My eyes blurry from tears, I told her we'd been close friends but I'd kept my crush on him hidden for fear of chasing him away. "Maybe he was warming up to me, though, because last month he said, 'Aww, you're moving out of the neighborhood,' when I told him I was buying a condo. But six months ago, after we went to a movie, he just shook my hand."

"Phooey on him," Lola smiled. "But that sure sounds like the Vic we knew and loved." She gestured toward a chair and handed me a tissue.

I sat, dabbing at my eyes. "He wasn't the least bit devious. When I told him I hated going to movies alone, I think he was clueless I was fishing for a date. Actually, I sort of twisted his arm."

"If he let you twist his arm, he wanted it twisted." Lola said. "My brother didn't let anyone make him do something against his will."

"Well, that's true. You know, the guys at the station called him the Incredible Hulk. But I thought of him as the Incredible Hunk."

"I'm sure he liked you too, more than you know," Lola said.

"Thank you." Her kindness to me in the face of her own sorrow touched me. Worrying my grief was intruding on theirs, I blinked rapidly, trying to push the tears back.

"Liz, there are some of Vic's things we specifically want you to have," Mike said.

"Oh, yes," Lola piped in. "Vic stored a hanging aquarium in his closet. It's just beautiful. Come see."

I agreed the porthole-shaped, ceramic aquarium was gorgeous. "Vic showed it to me but said he couldn't hang it because the pole for his gravity boots was installed in the only suitable spot."

"We'd ship it home except we're afraid it might break. It's so fragile," Lola explained. "And we want you to have Vic's shell chandelier and whatever albums and tapes you'd like. Pick what you want from the dishes, too."

I told Lola Vic had great taste, the aquarium and lamp would look lovely in my new condo, and I deeply appreciated their kindness. "I'll be able to keep a little bit of Vic around me now," I said, wondering if these lovely things could help drive away the loneliness waiting for me in the condo Vic would never see.

Lola asked me if I knew Norma, the seventy-something lady who lived in apartment 307. When I shook my head, she said Vic had told their parents Norma reminded him of his deceased grandmother, and baked him bread and goodies. "Norma told me Vic helped her out, took her places, and fixed things for her, ever since the death of her husband," Lola said, "Poor thing, she's so upset by this. Can I give you her phone number? She wants to meet you."

I copied Norma's number and invited Lola and Mike to lunch at my place on the following Thursday. They accepted, saying they would fly back to the mainland on the following day.

"One more thing before you go." Lola grabbed her address book. "We told my parents about you. My mother wants to write you. May I have your address?"

"Of course. I'd like yours, too, Lola."

We said our goodbyes. At the second floor landing, sadness seized me. I sat down and touched the banister on the spot Vic had touched it when he sat beside me the previous Halloween. "I feel like I've fallen into the darkest night, Vic," I whispered. "But I'm not traveling blind. Memories of you light my way."

***

On the following day, Vic's shift was on duty. Could it really be less than two weeks since his azure eyes closed forever? The gusting trade winds played quick rat-a-tat tunes on the fronds of the palm trees skirting the station's front lawn. The evening's tempo slugged along with only two routine F-4 fighter plane engine standbys and one downed power line.

The firemen and I talked for hours, our conversations turning around Vic and Jaku. I learned Jaku had bragged to every firefighter who'd listen about the crimes he'd committed. He'd told them everything he'd told me and more.

Since the firemen didn't know I'd been spilling my guts (well, some of them) to the detectives, they talked to me freely. When I asked them if they planned to tell Jet and Randy what Jaku had told them, they looked at me like I was batty. To a man, they agreed it wouldn't do any good to tell the cops what Jaku had said if the cops didn't already have enough evidence to convict him.

One fireman said, "It would only get me in hot water with management for not telling the chief earlier." Another remarked, "The chief's the one to blame. Why didn't he fire Jaku when Jaku slapped him?" A third said it was all hearsay evidence, and he didn't actually see Jaku commit any crimes.

Fear made the firemen shudder like dry drunks with the DTs. The worst case of the shakes belonged to The Skipper, our nickname for the crew chief on the huge P-15 truck he manned with Jaku. The Skip also slept in the same bunkroom as Jaku. A jittery fellow, he trembled at Jaku's stories about his criminal friends who drove a brown VW van and put the hurt on guys who "double crossed" Jaku.

"They're the same guys Jaku sent to beat up Ed Jones' mom and brothers," Skip told me, his rheumy eyes staring. On nights when Jaku was strung out on downers and too looped to respond to alarms, he obeyed Jaku's directive to cover for him even though he dripped sweat at the possibility of the fire chief finding out.

The rest of the crew knew about Jaku's absence as well, but no one reported him. When the P-15 rolled out of the station, the crew was often one man short. I was beginning to think Jaku was The Man, the way he ruled the station with fear, the way so many firemen kowtowed to him. They even saw him packing a loaded gun at the station and kept their lips zipped.

"I understand why you would tread lightly around Jaku," I told the Skipper. "I certainly did."

"I thought you'd understand," he said, warming up to me. "I ever tell you what he said after him and Vic fought in the truck stalls?"

"No." I'd heard about the fight, motivated by Jaku selling Vic a defective camera and Vic demanding his money back. Jaku's temper flared, and he threw punches at Vic, who simply held him at arm's length so he couldn't reach him with his wildly flailing arms. The guys chuckled about it among themselves, saying Jaku looked like a round clown, punching and missing. When Vic let him go, Jaku stomped into his bunkroom to vent.

"That asshole thinks he's big and bad," Jaku told the Skipper, "but I'm the guy gonna cut him down to size. You watch. One day, you watch."

"'I told Jaku, 'Don't talk like that. Don't even think it. Vic's your friend,'" the Skip said. "Jaku stormed out, but he must've thought about what I said 'cause he comes back an hour later and says, 'Yeah, you right, Skip. You right. I never mean it, yeah?' I told Jaku, 'Great.' And before I knew it, those two were friends again."

"Did you tell Vic what Jaku said?" I asked.

"Hell, no. Anyway, he must've known Jaku had a screw loose. Them two were buddies."

"Did you tell the detectives about the fight or about the brown VW van?" I asked.

"Are you crazy? No! And if you tell them what I said, I'll deny it!" His voice wobbled and his belly shook.

"Who said anything about telling the detectives?" I toyed with the idea. Maybe I should. Would they pressure the Skipper and the others to tell the truth like they'd pressured me?

"Jaku's a nut case. He's sneaky as a sidewinder and just as deadly. I ain't doing nothing that's gonna give him the idea of sending his punks after me, no way, no how, no never. Got it, Liz?" He glared at me.

"It's your decision. I understand. I know what fear feels like." I said, keeping my voice calm but seething inwardly at Vic's friends betraying him with their silences.

"I'm not afraid," he bristled. "I'm smart. I know how Jaku operates. Leave him alone, he'll leave you alone. You'd better be smart, too, if you know what's good for you."

Anger heated up my face, but I kept quiet. How could I blame him for adopting the same survival strategy I'd used all these years?

The most shocking news came from Sam Nobriga, a strapping, hard-drinking fireman. The previous December, Sam had gone nightclub hopping with Jaku and Vic. Afterward, the three of them shared a booth and wolfed down a midnight meal at some neon-lit, 24-hour restaurant.

They had just finished eating when Jaku nudged Sam and looked down. Sam followed Jaku's gaze and saw the gun Jaku was aiming at Vic under the table. A loaded gun, Jaku told Sam later, pointed at "That f . . . ing haole who thinks he's so big and bad but really ain't nothing but a f . . . ing haole." The freaky thing, Sam said, was the way Jaku acted like he was Vic's best pal, laughing and joking with him the whole time.

I pulled my jaw off the floor and said, "Did you tell Vic?"

Sam looked at me like I was nuts. "You know I couldn't. As straight ahead as Vic was, he would have confronted Jaku. Then my ass would have been grass. But I warned Vic to stay away from Jaku. After them two fought about the camera, I told Vic, 'Hey, man, Jaku's a nut case. Don't hang out with him. Don't do it.'"

Sam fell silent. I asked impatiently, "What did Vic say?"

"At first, nothing. He just kept wiping down his truck. Then he said with a deadpan face, 'Aww, he ain't so bad for a hot-tempered, gabby little dude. He can't help himself, being a perp and all'."

"So I said to Vic, 'Perp? Like in perpetrator of a crime?'"

"Vic answered, 'That and Puerto Rican Portuguese. Perp. A short name for shorty, don't you know?'"

Sam told me, "Perp was such a stellar name for Jaku, it made me laugh."

I said quietly, "Vic wouldn't have hung out with Jaku any more if he'd known about the gun. Couldn't you have found a way to tell him?"

"Vic knew Jaku had guns." Sam frowned. "He knew a lot more about him than we do. Don't forget, them two were running buddies. Hey, I'm not the one who killed Vic, sweetheart. Jaku was." He squinted at me and hurried away.

I was glad he was gone so I could voice my thoughts, "By keeping silent, you and some of the others tied Vic's hands and readied him for the kill. The only thing left for Jaku to do was pull the trigger."

* * *

The next morning, sunlight shining through my bedroom's open window pulled me out of a dark dream about Jaku's thugs slicing me with knives and chuckling as I screamed. Relieved to be awake, I flung the curtains open, savoring the sweet smell of mock orange blossoms on a hedge street-side of my red patio.

I told myself the nightmare was just showing me my fears. But my stomach cramped from the certainty that I would be the only one to testify regarding the crimes Jaku bragged about when I was his captive audience in the alarm room. Lino, Emilio, and Mike would testify as well, but only to say they'd seen Jaku bring a loaded gun to the station.

After Lino had told Chief Green about the gun, the chief pressured Emilio and Mike to talk. And they talked. Surely the firemen would do likewise, if I told Jet and he put the squeeze on them.

I dialed Homicide. Jet answered the phone. "Some of the firemen at work are withholding what they know about crimes Jaku committed," I told him. "Crimes he bragged to them about."

"Like what?"

"Like how he wrecked his car for the insurance money. Like how he and his thugs stole the station's entertainment center."

"So? When are they coming down to make a statement?"

"They won't. They're afraid of having to testify in court."

"Just wait until Jaku's out on the street again," Jet said, accentuating every word. "Then we'll see how afraid they'll be. Then they'll want to come down and talk to us, but it'll be too late. They expect the police to protect them, but they won't tell us the truth."

I shuddered at the thought of Jaku free to walk the streets. "I understand where they're coming from. You said you can't guarantee anyone protection 24 hours a day. And Jaku gets even with people."

"Think about what I just said." Jet sounded impatient, as if he were talking to a stubborn child. "Think about how you'll feel . . ." He stressed the word *you*, ". . . when Jaku's out on the street again."

My heart thumped painfully. "Why do you say that?"

"Is your conscience clear? If you haven't told us everything, you'll have to live with it for the rest of your life. You said Vic was like your brother. As long as you've told us the whole truth, don't worry about what Jaku told the others." Jet paused, waiting, I supposed, to see if I would speak. But I couldn't say a word. After a long silence he said, "I have to go."

I followed the click of his receiver with the slam of mine. "What good would it do anyway?" I yelled. "Vic's dead. Nothing I can say will bring him back. And if I go to court, Jaku will put the hurt on me, guaranteed! Jet Yamasato, you're a jerk!"

I kicked the couch leg, yelled, "*Owie*!" and rubbed my throbbing big toe. "*Owie*!" I yelled louder, more from frustration than pain. Fatigue forced me down on my bed and I slept.

I awoke with a start in the dark, hearing rain splattering against the windows, not knowing where I was. For a panic-stricken moment, I imagined I'd slept through work until I remembered I was off until the following morning. Thank god.

I felt my way through the dark bedroom to the kitchen, opened the refrigerator door, and grabbed a cold beer. Normally the most I drink is half a beer when I return home after midnight too wired to sleep. That's all it takes to knock me out.

But this night I drank to blot out thoughts about Jaku walking free,

Jet pressuring me, spineless firemen, and my own cowardice. And I wanted to numb the pain of missing Vic.

The second beer found me slumped in the overstuffed living room chair, one hand circling the can, the other pulling another tissue out of a box. Light seeping through an open window dimly lit the dark living room. I watched as the light chased ghost-like shadows across the wooden walls, and wished it could also chase my sadness away.

I thought about Vic's humor and generosity, and how hollow and cold my world had become with him gone. My eyes swelled and stung, and my stomach churned from the unaccustomed second beer. The rain sounded like bullets pinging against the window. I flashed on a blues line about the sky crying and tears rolling down my cheeks, and cried even harder.

The last thing I remember before falling into an exhausted sleep was feeling all hope had washed out of me along with my tears.

* * *

March came in like a gamboling lamb the next morning, with balmy weather and clear skies, but I felt like a grouchy lion. Drinking lots of water eased my throbbing head, and ice cubes on my eyelids reduced their swelling enough for me to wear my contact lenses to work.

Several years earlier, a friend in mourning told me work had become her refuge. I hadn't believed such a thing was possible until now. I welcomed the distraction from my grieving when work kept me busy with emergencies, reports, club closings, and routine refueling and engine start standbys.

But the fire station was a depressing place to be at other times, such as when I typed up the manning card and had to type a name other than Vic's as the Ramp 7 driver. Four days after Vic's death, tears blurred my vision even though Mad Max looked on and the last thing I wanted to do was cry in the presence of that iron man.

My fingers should have been striking the typewriter keys, spelling Vic's name, and Vic should have stuck his head into the alarm room after roll call, a big grin on his face, and asked, "Take a break, Snake?"

Max lightly placed a hand on my shoulder. "Are you all right, Liz?"

I answered between sobs, "It hit me hard just now . . . I won't type Vic's name as the ramp driver again. Not tomorrow, not next week, not ever."

"That's tough," he said. "That's real tough." After a long pause he added, "I'm sorry," before walking out into the crash stalls to inspect the work of the men wiping down the trucks. I'd never appreciated Mad Max as much as I did then, and resolved to think of him as Sergeant Maxwell from then on.

I did not, however, think kindly of some of the other firemen. I piled blame this sunny afternoon on Tim Thompson, merited, I believed, because of his abominable silence. Tim's charm and movie-star good looks attracted women by the score, but after he talked with me, he metamorphosed into an ugly man.

He told me he'd seen Jaku pointing a loaded .357 Magnum at Sergeant Maxwell's head several mornings when Max rode away on his bicycle. Tim described how Jaku yelled, "Boom!" and acted out pulling the trigger and feeling the recoil from the powerful weapon.

"How did you know the gun was loaded?" I asked.

"Duh!" Tim gave me a you-are-a-dumb-blonde look. "He showed me the bullets."

"Why was he mad . . . ?" I started to ask, but immediately knew the answer and had to change the question, "because Max kicked him out of the alarm room?"

"Right-o, Sherlock," Tim smirked.

I blurted out, "Well, Watson, did it ever occur to you to mention it to anybody? Say, like the chief?"

Tim looked at me like I was cuckoo. "Are you nuts? You know how Jaku is. He would have gotten even with me for sure."

I knew I should shut up but anger captured my tongue. "Even if you'd gone to the chief confidentially and sworn him to secrecy, and asked him to order a search of Jaku's belongings? Ever think of such a thing, or anything besides your own safety?"

"I don't have to stand here and take insults from a . . . a . . ." Tim's face flushed and his fist clenched, and for a moment I thought he would punch me in the face, "lame woman who's missing her lover and taking it out on an innocent guy."

"Vic wasn't my lover." *Innocent my ass.*

"So you say, but some say otherwise. Whatever. I don't care what you do. Anyway, I didn't kill Vic. Jaku did. And maybe you. Who knows what you and Vic and Jaku had going on?" He rubbed his chin in a teasing way but his eyes were angry.

I regretted losing my temper and with it any chance of getting more information from Tim. "Forgive me. Vic's death hit me hard, but I shouldn't take it out on you."

Tim mumbled something like "forget it" and hurried from the room.

I decided it was dumb and judgmental to blame Tim or anyone else who didn't feel an emotional tie to Vic. I had come forward only because I cared about Vic and realized our friendship obligated me to tell the truth about Jaku. Jet was obviously hip to this and knew how to get to me. His words, "You must tell the truth for Vic. You said he was like a brother to you. Won't you tell the truth for your brother?" still bounced and echoed through my mind.

Two mornings later, on a stormy Sunday, clouds blotted out the sunrise, leaving only a gray and overcast dawn. I couldn't bear to stay in my condo's silent rooms and think the same agitated thoughts over and over.

My plan had been to drive up Aiea Heights Drive and walk along streets canopied with golden shower trees, past stately homes bordered by crimson hibiscus flower bushes. But the lack of sunshine sent me to a nearby nursery instead, to search for a plant to replace the marigolds dying on my patio despite my best efforts to revive them.

Rain poured through the nursery's open ceiling, spattering off my rain bonnet, flowing in little rivulets down my neck. I retreated to the perimeter of the courtyard of plants where a tin roof protruding from the building's brick walls shielded me as I walked around the outskirts of the courtyard.

A short brunette with a yellow nametag pinned to her blue uniform shirt approached me and asked if she could help me find anything.

"Just looking."

She returned to her cash register, leaving me alone with my thoughts, the only customer in the large building.

I savored the colors and shapes and smells filling the nursery. The hypnotic dripping of raindrops on leaves soothed me, and serenity overtook me as I ambled along. Then I spotted it—a plant six inches high with green leaves and clusters of fuzzy purple flowers. A twin of the one I had given Vic when I visited him in the hospital.

Memories overtook me of Vic joking and laughing with me, teasing me, standing up for me, confiding in me. The memories touched me deeply. At the same time, I felt Vic as an unseen presence. I had sensed his presence before, his joyful essence like sunlight on water, sparkling and free, but this time was different. This time his soul cried out as if his heart had been hit by a cannonball. I could not believe this was really happening; me feeling his grief and it instantly becoming mine.

Hot tears streamed down my cheeks. Was the stress of losing Vic making me crack up? Was this what insanity felt like? I tried grabbing onto something concrete to rescue me from this grief. Not knowing what else to do, I bowed my head and asked God to point a way out of this storm.

The answer came immediately, like an indictment from heaven, like an inner voice. But this voice did not sound like the jagged self-talk I usually heard inside my head. No, this voice spoke slowly and deeply and sounded like Vic's voice saying, "You didn't tell the whole truth for me."

I gasped as the implications of those eight words washed over me. Oh, dear god. Vic would never have allowed fear to stop him from telling the whole truth for me. Jet was right. I should have told him everything.

A hand on my shoulder made me jump. I spun around to face the worried frown of the cashier. She asked hesitantly, "You all right, Miss?"

I nodded, speechless, and ran as quickly as I could from the nursery through the drenching rain. After flinging my front door open, I rushed inside and immediately dialed Homicide.

Against all odds, Jet was there, tidying up some paperwork, he said, from one of his umpteen cases. "What's up, Liz?" His manner was conversational and friendly.

I trembled, anticipating his anger when he learned my testimony had been less than complete. Fear seized me and my mind flailed around for some convincing excuse to hang up. I wished I could at least hint at the stupendous event transpiring in the nursery while he was caught up in paperwork, but the only words spilling out of my mouth were, "I didn't tell you everything."

His tone of voice changed instantly. "Like what?" he demanded.

In one long breath, I told him, "Jaku told me he cut Deputy Chief Henderson's brake lines; he told me he had the soldier's family beaten up. He said he set fire to his car in the cane fields so he could collect the insurance money. And he told me things he might do in the future—set fire to the station; put a bomb in the chief's office." I gasped for air and felt relieved I'd gone through with it.

"The defense attorney will say you came to us four times, that you are not a credible witness." Jet's voice was stiff with anger.

Ashamed of my cowardice and chastised by his anger, I whispered, "I am terrified of being the only one to testify. Jaku told those stories to everybody."

Some of the anger faded from Jet's voice. "I can't see you today."

"I'm off tomorrow until 3 p.m."

"Nine o'clock Monday, then." Jet banged the receiver down.

I searched my bookcases for enough blank paper to hold all I had to say about my three and a half years working with Vic and Jaku.

* * *

The following morning, for the third time, I sat on the hard wooden bench across the hall from the Homicide Division. The door beside the reception counter opened and I returned Jet's unsmiling stare. Neither of us spoke as I followed him down a narrow hallway to a tiny interview room.

We faced each other across a vinyl card table, his gaze as cold as the icy temperature of the room. I shivered. As before, a tape recorder rested on the table between us.

Without a word, I handed him ten handwritten, legal-sized pages of lined yellow notebook paper.

"What's this?" he snapped.

I answered softly, "I wrote it all down."

He quickly thumbed through the pages, counting them, noticing they were written on front and back. "We won't need this, then," he said, nodding at the tape recorder. His voice was gentler than before and I imagined he appreciated not having to interview such a headstrong witness.

He started reading my statement:

> *I've gotten my fear under control now. The worst thing that can happen is Jaku sending his criminal friends after me when he hears what I have to say about him in court. Like he did to Ed Jones' family after Ed turned him in to the Security Police for smoking pot in the bunkrooms.*
>
> *I am part of the triangle of Jaku and Vic because I was attracted to Vic, Jaku was attracted to me, and the two of them were friends. Even if you draw lines between our three apartments, it forms a triangle; each of us living only a few blocks from the other two.*

He pursed his lips, nodded, and continued reading.

> *Sometimes Jaku invited me over to his apartment. I used my boyfriend Billy as an excuse not to go. Jaku thought I was cool to have a local boyfriend.*

He asked, "Did Jaku and Billy know each other?"

"No."

He resumed reading.

I had written about every significant incident occurring between Jaku, Vic, and me during the three and a half years we worked together. How Jaku told sexual lies about me but Brian Smith warned me not to confront him. How I pretended to be Jaku's friend and listened, wide-eyed, when he pummeled me with his true crime stories. How Vic and Jaku were pals but Vic seemed to be blind to Jaku's dark side.

I described how Jaku's stories changed from true crime to graphic sexual conquests after the news of Vic's and my double date circulated through the station. How I had Jaku kicked out of the alarm room during his temporary promotion to captain for telling me graphically obscene stories. How, ten days later, before Thanksgiving, management permanently promoted someone else to captain. How, ten days later, before Thanksgiving, management permanently promoted someone else to captain.

I wrote about my last conversation with Jaku on December 30th, the day before he took leave for two weeks. I described how Jaku called in sick for four more weeks after that, and how the day he shot Vic was the day he either had to come back to work or be fired.

I wrapped up my statement with these words:

> In those last six weeks before he was killed, while Jaku was on leave, Vic seemed to shake himself free of Jaku's dark influence. Vic and I laughed until our sides ached. We talked long and intensely. I'm grateful for those times we shared but I miss him terribly.

I sat quietly, my chin resting in my hands, and watched as Jet read page after page of my written words. For the first time in a long time I felt relaxed, my conscience finally clear.

A loud thought popped into my mind, like a radio broadcast but spoken in Jet's utterly authoritative voice: *This man wanted to rape Liz.* The voice was so clear I looked at Jet to see if he had spoken the words, but his attention was riveted on the pages.

Had I really picked up Jet's thought, or was stress making me hear voices existing only in my mind? Shivering, I said, "It sure is cold in here."

"It sure is." Jet didn't look up. After reading the last page of my statement, he placed the sheets of paper on the table beside him, raised an eyebrow and said, surprise in his voice, "This is what you wanted to tell the police?"

I nodded and wondered what he had expected.

"Your statement is very complete. Some of this you told me before, but that's all right."

"I wanted to tell you everything this time."

"It's in the hands of the police now, Liz." His voice was kind. "Now, I'd like you to initial each page."

Jet placed the sheets of paper in front of me one page at a time. As I wrote LH on each one, I felt his intense gaze boring into me. When I finished, he said, "I'll hold onto these, if I may. Thank you for coming down."

"You're welcome." I wanted to apologize for not telling him everything earlier but the words formed a lump in my throat. Silently, I followed him down the narrow hallway and out Homicide's front door. Neither of us spoke as I turned and walked away.

That evening, frantic and irate phone calls tied up the switchboard after a broken water main flooded dozens of ground floor apartments. Despite the agitation of the night, the serenity that had washed over me after I told Jet my whole truth remained.

The following morning, sunlight angling through my living room window illuminated a stack of Vic's record albums shoved under the couch.

The names of many of the musicians were familiar but most of the albums were not. I played a few Stevie Wonder and Chuck Mangione songs and swayed to the music. But when I read the deep-hearted lyrics of Steve Winwood's "Arc of a Diver" album, they seemed like they'd been written expressly for Vic and me.

I played the album on my old turntable. The driving rock and roll music had me dancing, love flowing through me as Steve sang about warm water breathing, feeling your lover near, circling all around.

Italiano, you still entice me. "Slow down, sundown," Steve sang, "Here's to all the strong ones who don't care if they win, the kind we'll never see again." I thought, *Great heart, your sun set way too soon.*

A gusting south wind blew a hard rain against my living room window. Although I'd shut the louvers so water wouldn't blow in, a cool breeze sprang up and swirled through the room, making my wind chimes bounce, the dancing rods tinkling melodically.

How strange and wonderful, for the wind to enter in with the windows closed. Suddenly, somehow, I knew this was no earthly wind. No, this was the breath of God. This was the sparkling energy essence of Vic Lazzarini. *Oh please, Lord. Let me breathe him in just one more time.*

I turned into a human sponge, absorbing Vic's unique blend of playfulness and joy as his essence seemed to soak through my every cell. The air vibrated with consciousness and joy, the wind swirled, caressing me as I danced to the music. My heart became warm and then hot as I merged with the energy penetrating me, deeply connected to Vic and, at the same time, wildly free.

As suddenly as it arose, the wind died down and Vic was gone. I sank to the carpet, hugging myself, trying to hold onto the ecstasy. When mundane awareness seeped back into me, I found comfort in knowing I'd said yes to the wild energy, and my memories could always transport me back.

* * *

The following morning, my real estate agent phoned with welcome news. The condo I was buying would close in eleven days, a month earlier than anticipated. I phoned my parents, and gratefully accepted my mother's offer to fly to Hawai'i and help me set up house.

I carried a dozen mildewed, spider-webbed boxes from their storage place beneath my stairwell. Five o'clock, time for my pre-midnight shift nap, found me still sorting through my stuff and thinking about that rainy January afternoon when I told Vic I would be buying a condo.

"The interest rate's only ten percent, so I'll be paying about five hundred a month. Including the maintenance fee—just fifty-six dollars." I smiled. "Cheapest on Oahu."

Vic said wistfully, "Aww. You're moving out of the neighborhood."

Charmed that he thought of the high-rise, high-crime district of Makiki where we lived as a neighborhood, and delighted that he cared I was moving away, I took a risk, saying, "But I won't be too far away to visit friends. And I'll throw a housewarming party—if you'll come."

Something flashed in his eyes. I worried about overstepping his boundaries until he smiled and said, "That's cool, that's cool."

The memory of the look in his now lifeless eyes made me sob. I tried to sleep but couldn't. I was so tired of riding a roller coaster of agony and ecstasy. The midnight shift found me struggling to stay awake, and wondering why I had to go through all of this.

***

On Friday, March 8, I drove to Vic's apartment building and introduced myself to Norma Walker, a sharp-witted, seventy-something woman who'd been like a grandmother to Vic. She stood five foot five to my five eight and gave me the once over with sparking blue eyes. "Come right in, dear," she said. "Please call me Norma." She gestured toward a tan and cream-colored couch I recognized as Vic's.

I sat on the couch and she settled into a straight-backed chair with an embroidered cushion. "Lola, that poor dear, gave me the couch you're sitting on," Norma said. "I feel like Vic's sitting beside me every time I sit there. Oh, how I miss that kid. He was just like a grandson to me. He used to smell the bread I baked and he'd walk down the stairs and knock on my door and say, 'Do I smell something good coming from down here?' He'd sniff the air and of course I'd give him a loaf, the big tease."

I smiled. "Vic told me about you and the delicious bread you baked."

"I always baked extra goodies for Vic. Oh, how I loved that kid! To have him shot by that little worm Jaku is just too horrible."

"Yes, totally horrible," I agreed. "I'll never get over losing Vic either."

"He was so good looking. My sister used to say, 'He's such a doll.' And I'd say, 'You call that big man a doll?' But he was a sweetheart and so good to me. You don't find many young folks who are courteous toward old people these days." Tears brimmed in her eyes. "After my husband died last September, Vic always asked me if I needed a ride or any kind of help. Such a considerate young man."

I told her Vic was my dear friend, too, and work felt like a morgue without him.

"You're nice and tall and pretty, too," Norma said. "Were you Vic's girlfriend?"

I told her no but I had wanted to be and maybe would have been if we'd had more time.

She nodded. "You would have made an attractive couple. Oh, it's so nice to meet someone who loved Vic the way I did!"

She gave me a loaf of delicious-smelling, freshly-baked banana bread. We traded phone numbers and agreed to keep in touch.

When I arrived home, a letter from Vic's mom awaited me. I sat at my kitchen table, nibbled on Norma's bread, and read:

Dear friend of Vic's,

> *We can't really write what we feel at this time over losing our son Vic, but Lola told us about meeting you and you and Vic were good friends. I'm glad he had an extra sister over there to look up to and we thank you for being a friend of his.*
>
> *We will really miss him and his phone calls home, and just to hear his voice made our day when he called. He was such a wonderful son and we loved him and were always so proud of him. We have only happy and wonderful memories of him.*
>
> *We had a Memorial Service for him at our church where he was baptized. He had many friends here even though he didn't get home often. It was just April of last year he was here with us and I still can't accept it he is gone and I know I never will. A part of us will always be over in Hawai'i. God has been our strength and such a comfort to us, and we are so thankful for the prayers of our friends and loved ones.*

I know Vic is in God's hands and enjoying all the blessings God has promised each of us but it's hard to accept. I keep asking Him, "Why, Lord? Why Vic?" I can almost hear Vic saying, "I'm okay, Mom. I'm free, like a bird." He told me, when he rode his motorcycle here at home (he would go riding out on the country roads) that he felt free like a bird.

I always told him he was my favorite son. He would laugh and say, "I'm your only son," and on the birthday cards and Mother's Day cards he always signed them, "Your favorite son" or "Your sunshine kid," and I look at them now and know he was the sunshine of my life, besides our daughters Lola and Betty and their families.

Forgive me for telling you all this, but after Lola told me what a wonderful girl you were I feel like I have known you before this. May God richly bless you and keep you in a very special way, and thank you again for being one of Vic's friends and adopted sister.

Sincerely,
Vic's Mom & Dad

I laid my head on the kitchen table and cried.

* * *

On swing shift that evening, between phone calls and standbys, I wrote Vic's parents a letter, promising to write or call the moment I learned anything new. I had just signed my name when five firemen descended on the adjoining assistant chief's office to talk and smoke. I closed the door to shut out the fumes.

When dinner time arrived, Tony knocked softly on the alarm room door. "Are you escaping from cancer sticks behind closed doors?" he asked.

"Yes. And remembering things I'd rather forget." I said yes to the break he offered and asked, "Did you find out anything about Jaku's bail at yesterday's bail hearing?

"Bail's still set at fifty grand. The prosecutor's office said the same thing as Chief Green—that's unusually high for a murder case." Tony frowned. "But, since Jaku shot Vic four times at close range, seems like it ought to be at least a hundred grand."

"It ought to be a million. Surely we don't need to worry, though. No way Jaku could come up with fifty thousand."

"He'd only have to pay ten percent—five grand—in cash. The rest would be collateral, if he could put up something worth that much. Like his parents' house."

"You're kidding!" I shuddered at the thought. "But Jaku's mom said her husband wasn't backing Jaku, right?"

Tony nodded. "So maybe they won't put their house up for him."

"Let's hope not." I stood so Tony could take my place at the console.

"Indeed." Tony plopped down. "What's to stop Jaku from coming out here and shooting some of us now that he's already a murderer and has nothing more to lose?"

Chapter 7

Monday, March 11, through Wednesday, March 26

After working the Sunday mid shift, my head hit the pillow at 8:30 a.m. The next morning. I was still sleeping at 4:30 p.m. when the phone rang. Struggling to wake up, I grabbed the receiver.

"Liz, this is Judy, from work." Her normally calm voice sounded nervous.

"What's up?" I yawned. "I don't work 'til midnight."

"The chief said to call you and tell you Jaku's out on bail."

This news shocked me awake. "Oh, no! When did he get out?"

"About half an hour ago."

I could barely choke out the words, "How awful!"

"Yes, I know. Jaku's parents put up their house for him. The chief got a call from the security police, who got a call from a prison guard downtown. Jaku was just released to his parents' custody."

"Th . . . th . . . thanks for telling me." My hand shook so badly I could barely place the receiver back in its cradle. Jaku, out. Free, right now.

I phoned Homicide. Jet answered. I blurted out, "Jaku's out!"

"Oh? He made bail? No one told me. Who told you?"

My voice wobbled. "Judy, a dispatcher. Chief Green asked her to call me."

Jet didn't say a word. A minute dragged by. I broke the silence, sobbing, "I'm scared!"

"Liz." Jet's voice was hard, stern. "Live your life. If he bothers you, call the police."

"Okay," I whispered. *As if I would have a chance to call the police.* But I didn't dare voice a thought contradicting the word of The Law. Indeed, I hardly breathed, immobilized as I was by fear.

I thought about Vic, how he stood no chance against a man with no conscience. I thought about Jaku, probably forced to live with his parents now but knowing where I lived. Well, I wasn't going to let him sneak up on me in the dark. I would stay with friends until my new condo closed, and come back to my apartment to pack during the day.

I dialed my friend Carey. She and her sergeant husband lived on Whaler which, I reasoned, offered some protection because a sticker was needed to drive on base. I asked her if I could hang out at her place later, maybe take a nap before work.

"Of course you can," Carey said. "And you can spend the night when you're not working, except for a few nights when we'll have guests."

"You are a true friend." My teeth chattered. "I'll never forget it."

When I broke the connection, I felt broken, too, and curled up on my bed in a fetal position. My mind flailed around in a quicksand of fearful thoughts, including that it was madness to lie here when Jaku might kick the door open at any moment.

I decided to call my parents and tell them where they could reach me at night. *Stay cool. You don't want to upset them.* Even after several deep breaths, I couldn't stop shaking.

"But Liz," my father said, "I still don't see why that man would want to bother you. You have told us everything, haven't you? Is there something you're holding back?"

"Dad," I tried to keep my voice steady, "we think he was coming to work Valentine's Day morning to kill people. Who knows what he'll do now? Remember, I had him kicked out of the alarm room. He knows where I live. I'm not staying here alone at night. I'll stay at Carey's or other friends' homes for the next six nights until I move."

"You go right ahead and stay at Carey's if it makes you feel better," Mom said.

I felt guilty at the worry in her voice, and told her I was undoubtedly overreacting. "I have a tendency for high drama," I said, "but I come by it honestly. Just look at Dad."

She laughed and my father said, "Oh ho, ho, ho, Miss Smarty Pants," which made me feel better. I gave them Carey's phone number, and wrote down the address and phone number of dad's business partner, Mark Hamilton.

"I already called Mark and told him about the nut case you worked with," Dad said. "You can stay at his house. He talked it over with his wife and its fine with her."

"They have an extra bedroom," Mom added. "So you just give them a call if things don't work out for you to stay at Carey's house every night."

"And give us a call tomorrow," Dad said.

I promised I would, and thanked them for being the best parents on the planet.

Even though I knew I should grab my work stuff and get out, fear froze me. A sudden idea, to talk to a priest, got me moving again. I'm not Catholic. But, in my terrified state of mind, a priest seemed like the most powerful link to God.

I phoned a nearby Catholic church.

"St. John's Directory," a woman answered, her voice loudly bureaucratic.

"I must speak to a priest. It's urgent. Right now, if I could, please."

"Just a moment." A long silence followed before the woman said, "You may come and speak with Father Daniels for a few minutes. But he leaves in half an hour."

"I'll be right there."

Father Daniels was fifty-something, stocky, with white hair and a kind face. "What's wrong?" He watched my tears trickle down my cheeks.

"A demon has come into my life." Briefly, I told him about Jaku shooting Vic.

"Do the police know about all this?" the priest asked.

I nodded.

"Well, I believe in demons," he said. "But I also believe in God. Do you believe in God?"

"Yes."

"God is stronger."

The conviction is his voice reassured me.

"Now, I want you to visualize a huge tree in your mind's eye, with deep roots and branches reaching into the heavens."

I closed my eyes.

"Do you see it?"

"Yes."

"What you see is the Tree of Life," the priest said, "God's tree. This is God's world, and fear is the great destroyer. You can't live with the extreme fear you are feeling now. Trust in the Lord, and He will protect you. Have faith."

I nodded and breathed deeply.

He added, "Now, I want you to say the Lord's Prayer with me. Then I will bless you with this holy oil, and you will be under God's protection."

We prayed together. Father Daniels dipped his finger into a small vial filled with yellow liquid. He rubbed a cross of oil on my forehead, handed me the vial, and said, "Keep this Chrism oil with you. It has been blessed and will protect you. Any time fear overtakes you, rub this oil on your forehead and pray for the Lord to protect you."

"Thank you." *And if I die, at least I will be in a state of grace.*

Driving toward Whaler beneath the night sky ablaze with stars, I felt calmer than before, my hands steadier on the wheel.

Carey's front door stood ajar. My godchild, three-year-old, auburn-haired Peggy, ran to me on chubby legs. "Mommy! Auntie Liz!" the little girl squealed.

"Give Auntie a kiss." I sat beside Carey at the kitchen table, her child in my arms.

"Peggy just had her bath," Carey smiled. "She's ready to go night-night."

"No, Mommy!" Peggy protested, clinging tightly to me. She started to cry.

"Oh, all right. You can stay up for ten minutes and visit with Auntie Liz." Peggy played with my earring. "Care for coffee, Liz, or would you rather nap first?"

"Coffee, please. I just hope it doesn't make me shakier than I already am," I said. "I even went to see a priest just now."

"Why? You're not Catholic."

"Somehow, a priest seemed like the most direct channel to God." I shrugged. "Who knows? Years ago, a clairvoyant palmist said I was a Catholic nun in a former life."

Carey shared my belief in reincarnation. "Could be."

We talked until I left for work shortly before midnight. When I arrived at the fire station, Judy told me the firemen had checked out all keys to the bunkrooms. "Everyone locked themselves in for the night. That way, if Jaku comes out here, at least he won't be able to walk in on anybody unannounced."

"It's going to be real cute if they respond to an emergency," I said. "They'll rush to their doors and won't be able to open them. Then they'll yell, 'Who's got the damned key?' There'll be a chaotic scramble. I can see it now."

Judy laughed. "Yeah, or if somebody wakes up and has to go to the bathroom, they'll have to wake up whoever's got the key. But I totally understand how they feel. They're scared out of their wits."

I nodded. "They sound like me. Tonight I'll turn the lights low so nobody can see in, and keep a close watch on this place."

* * *

The next morning, the jangling phone jarred me awake after three hours' sleep. My disgruntled "Hello" was followed by Tony's, "Thought you'd want to know Jaku just came on base."

My sleepiness evaporated. "Sure do!"

Jaku had driven to the main gate, told the Security Police who he was, and said he needed to go to the credit union. The cops scraped his base sticker, escorted him there and back, then phoned Sergeant Maxwell and told him what Jaku had said. "Jaku was rattling on the whole time," Tony said, "talking nonstop; you know how he does."

"What did he say?"

"That he was innocent, and Vic came at him with a gun, and was getting in the way of Jaku and the girl Jaku wanted to marry. Jaku told the S.P.s he'd saved up five grand for the wedding but now he had to spend it on a lawyer."

"Sounds like lies and more lies to me," I said. "Where does he get this stuff?"

"Beats the hell out of me. Get a load of this. He tells the cops he called his friends at the fire station and they'd all forgiven him." I snorted and Tony said, "Yeah, I know. And he told them, 'Hey, man, I'm gonna be back at work in a couple of months, when this thing gets cleared up, you watch.' Mind you, the cops didn't ask him a single question."

"Unreal. We all forgave him, huh? Sounds like he's off the deep end."

"My thoughts exactly," Tony said. "No telling what he'll say or do next."

"You suppose Jaku might get off if he pleads insanity?" I shuddered at the thought.

"The possibility worries me. I'd like to find out if the trial's still set for June 9th so we'll know how long he'll be free." An alarm tone wailed in the background. "Got to go. Mind calling Jet or Randy? They should know."

Despite my embarrassment at my loss of control the night before, I said I would. I dialed the police department. Answering Jet's brusque "Homicide," with a subdued, "Liz speaking," I asked, "Do you know if the trial date for Jaku is still set for June 9?"

"No," Jet said gently. "Liz, I don't think you folks have anything to worry about."

I whispered, "You don't?" *Unbelievable.*

"No. By the way, we didn't know he was out. You're the only one who told me."

"Oh, he's out, all right. He came on base today." My voice trembled.

"Jaku doesn't know what you told us," Jet assured me.

"That makes me feel better." I breathed deeply. "I didn't know. I don't really know how the system works. I heard there were several bail hearings but—"

Jet interrupted, "Jaku won't know until the trial."

I wondered if I would be safe until then but only asked, "Who can I call to find out the date of the trial?"

Jet said the prosecutor's office might know.

The prosecutor's secretary connected me to the deep, authoritative voice of the Deputy Prosecutor. "Paul Zimmerman," he said. "How can I help you?"

"Hello. My name is Liz, and I'm a dispatcher at Whaler Fire Department and—"

"Oh? Is there a fire?" I laughed politely. He asked if I was one of the people worrying about the firefighter who just made bail.

"Yes. We think he was coming to work that morning to kill the chiefs."

After a long pause, Zimmerman said, "Well, the man certainly is a belligerent individual. If it's any consolation to you, these criminals rarely repeat a crime. They know they're being watched and the first wrong move will land them back in jail."

"Oh, will he be under police surveillance, then?"

"No one will be specifically assigned to tail him, if that's what you mean."

"What are the conditions of bail?"

"Mr. Cardoza was released on what is termed a *lis pendens*. His parents pledged their house for the fifty-thousand-dollar bail. Their home is appraised at a hundred and twenty thousand, with no liens or encumbrances. In other words, it's paid off. If he doesn't show up for the trial, his parents lose their entire home, not just the fifty grand. He had to put up five thousand in cash."

"Do you know if the trial is still set for the week of June 9th?"

"Let's see." A long pause followed. "Yes, it is. However, what with the enormous backlog, dates get postponed. You can call back on

March 20th and have my secretary check the new schedule."

I thanked him. Wide awake and sure further sleep was impossible, I resumed packing. Doing something physical soothed my frazzled nerves, so I kept at it.

Rain pinged against my windows. The repetitive *plop, plop, plop* of water dripping off the roof and the cool air lulled me. The phone rang. A click was the only answer to my "Hello." My mind screamed "Jaku!" and my hand shook as I slammed the receiver down. I dialed Carey and asked her if I could come over right away.

"Oh, sure," that angel said.

Five minutes later, I slung a backpack stuffed with work clothes and snacks over my shoulders. I locked the door behind me and nervously scanned the neighborhood. Could a murderer be hiding in the weed-choked vacant lot behind my apartment?

I shook like a drunk with the DTs as I sprinted to my car.

Again I surveyed the area, the cars speeding down Ward Avenue, the people holding umbrellas and walking along the sidewalk in front of my landlord's house.

Driving past Jaku's apartment on the way to the freeway, I noticed his black Toyota was missing from the open garage. I hoped he had to stay with his parents on the windward side. As my car inched through bumper-to-bumper traffic, I wondered if Jaku had been high on drugs the morning he killed Vic.

* * *

The following day, after taping up my last cardboard box, I drove *makai*, toward the white-capped ocean lapping at the pier at the end of Ward Avenue. On this sticky afternoon, the trade winds blew from the steamy south rather than the usual cool northeast. Sweat dripped down my forehead.

I headed to a nearby shopping center to go dumpster diving for more boxes. When the traffic light at Kapiolani Boulevard turned red, I pressed my foot to the brake pedal until it hit the floor. My car did not slow down.

Panicked, I grabbed the emergency brake. The car screeched to a halt. My heart racing, I drove four blocks to my usual car repair shop. The mechanic humored my request to check my brake lines to see if they'd been cut with a knife the same way Jaku had cut Deputy Chief Bob's brakes. Only after the mechanic told me the brakes were intact did I remember Jet's words, "Jaku won't know what you told us until the trial." I breathed deeply and relaxed.

Since I needed my car to get to work that night, the manager agreed to squeeze in the brake job and finish by 5 p.m. But I had to leave the car and walk nine hot blocks home in my flip-flops. Blisters formed where the straps rubbed between my toes. I felt sorry for myself—the blisters, the unexpected repair bill, and now how would I ever find boxes today? The sun sizzled on my neck. I prayed for help.

Back in my apartment, I called two girlfriends and asked if they could drive me around to look for boxes, but both were busy. I asked the retired couple next door the same question, but they were heading out.

"I understand," I said for the third time, biting my lip to hold back tears. My neighbors shut their door. *What now? I sure could use a helping hand.*

Blisters burning, I walked a short distance back to my front door. Following an impulse, I took a few more steps for a clear view of Ward Avenue. My gaze came to rest on an old brown two-story apartment building directly across the street.

A large, open garage filled the street-level area of the building. Something bulky was piled up high against the back wall. I squinted and gasped, first in disbelief, then in delight. A tower of at least 30 large, empty boxes leaned against the wall. Thirty boxes! Cardboard manna from heaven indeed.

A feeling of joy shot through me like electricity running through a lamp. The air around me seemed to shimmer, not with heat, but with consciousness. I laughed and felt Vic near.

Others fail me but you never do, Vic. Not even now. Thank you, God.

Cautiously, I crossed the busy street. The boxes were stained with produce, but intact. It occurred to me I should ask someone if I could take the boxes. But the garage was empty, I didn't know who to ask, and who was I to question the providence of Heaven?

I decided those boxes had my name on them. One of them actually did; Liz was written in big black letters across the side. Soon half of them were stacked in my living room. I wiped them down and packed like a woman possessed.

Later that night, over a cup of tea, I told Carey what happened. "I think I'm under protection. I felt Vic's presence today."

Carey nodded. "Well, you asked for protection. And the Bible says all you have to do is ask."

* * *

At two o'clock on the following morning, I locked the alarm room to prevent unannounced visits from drunks who sometimes stumbled into the station from a nearby military airline terminal. I also dimmed the lights to prevent firemen on their way to the john from looking through the one-way glass and seeing me cry.

My tears turned the small red, yellow and green lights shining in the black surfaces of the instrument panels into blurry circles. *The firemen won't tell the truth for Vic even though they called him friend.* Placing my elbows on the console and covering my face with my hands, I sobbed. Could it really be only four weeks since Vic died? It seemed like four years.

The door creaked open in the adjoining office. A line of light shone underneath the alarm room door. I looked through the peephole into Deputy Chief Bob's sleepy face and opened the door.

"Why did you turn the lights down?" he asked curtly.

I knew he thought I'd been sleeping. But as his eyes became accustomed to the dim light he asked, "What's wrong?" and then, "Can I help?"

I sniffled. "Some of the guys saw Jaku pointing a loaded gun at Sergeant Maxwell and Vic. Others heard Jaku brag about his thug friends putting the hurt on guys who crossed him. But nobody will breathe a word of this to the cops."

Bob leaned against the door. "I've called the entire shift into the training room several times, asking anyone who knows anything incriminating about Jaku to please come forward." He frowned. "But no one has. Do you know if anybody's heard from Jaku?"

I shrugged. "Maybe me. Every day since Jaku made bail, the phone rings, but when I say hello, the caller hangs up without a word. I'm glad I'm moving in three days. Still okay to use your van on Sunday?"

"Sure," Bob grinned, "providing it's running at the time."

"Great. Seven guys said they'd help me move. I told them I'll have pizza and beer waiting."

Bob shook his head. "Better hide the booze until the work's done, or you'll never get moved."

* * *

The next morning, I walked down the police station's cigarette butt-littered hallway to the wooden counter fronting the Homicide Division. A woman looked up from her desk and asked, "Can I help you?"

"I'm here to see Detective Yamasato," I said.

She glanced at a desk calendar and frowned. "Do you have an appointment?"

"No," I admitted. "But I phoned a few times and left a message. I know he's very busy, but it's important I talk with him."

She dialed a number, spoke too softly for me to hear, and said, "Please have a seat. Jet will be out shortly."

The door behind the woman's cubicle opened. Randy stepped out, his arms full of papers, and sat beside me. In response to my "How are you?" he said, "Too busy. We don't have time to finish the paperwork for one case before the next one crops up."

I nodded.

He added, "Right now we've got five cases we're working on."

The door opened again. Jet leaned against the doorframe, crossed his arms across his chest, and in a clipped voice demanded, "Yes?"

I blurted out, "One of the firemen at work saw Jaku point a loaded gun at Sergeant Maxwell's head, several mornings, when he rode away on his bicycle."

Randy stood up. "What's this fireman's name?" he asked.

"Tim Thompson. And another fireman saw Jaku point a loaded gun at Vic under the table when the three of them went nightclubbing." My heart pounded like a sledgehammer, "And a bunkmate of Jaku's heard Jaku threaten to send these criminal friends of his after a guy who'd crossed him—"

Jet interrupted, "So when are Tim and these other two men going to come in and tell us about it?"

"They won't. They're too scared."

Randy glanced at his watch and walked away.

Jet frowned. "Lino says it might have been the same gun. Emilio and Mike say they can't be sure. They're all panty over there; is that what you're trying to tell us, Liz?"

"Yes. They're panty." Instantly I regretted my smug tone of voice.

Jet's eyes narrowed. "Oh, yeah? What about you? Four times you came to us!"

My face grew hot. "I know," I said in a small voice. "I was scared, too. Still am."

"I told you before, I can't use secondhand information." Jet glared at me. "You telling me what Tim saw doesn't do the police any good. Tim has to tell us."

"But Tim told me. Won't that do?" Stubbornly, I held on to hope.

"No!" Jet's jaw clenched. "I told you, we don't accept secondhand information!"

But mine was secondhand. Hearsay, every bit of it, because I didn't actually see Jaku perform the crimes he bragged about. In the face of Jet's anger, I didn't dare voice these thoughts. Instead, I asked, "Well, then, why don't you ask Tim? He won't lie to you. You're the police."

Jet squinted at me. "You lied to us," he accused.

His words stunned me. "I didn't lie to you."

He shook his head and hissed, "Tsk, tsk, tsk" through his teeth.

My cheeks burned as I admitted, "I didn't tell you everything right away."

"A lie of omission!" Jet declared.

"But I did tell you everything, finally." I wished I could sink into the ground, away from Jet's indignation. "Even though it took me four times to tell all of it."

"Why did it take you so long?" Jet pressed. "I told you fear was just fear."

I remembered Jet saying, "Are you going to stop taking showers because most accidents occur in the tub?" But I considered my fear of being killed far more intense than the fear bathers experienced taking a shower. Words to spell out what I was thinking escaped me. The only ones I could summon up were, "It's not the same."

My answer seemed to enrage him. "Fear is just fear!" he insisted. I struggled to find words to explain but couldn't, and blinked back tears, and wondered why he was coming down so hard on me.

If his gentler tone of voice was an indication, Jet understood how I felt. "No, Liz," he said. "The information you're bringing me today, I can't use. It's secondhand. We don't operate like that. We don't coerce people who aren't willing to come to us."

The change in his manner toward me gave me the courage to voice my thoughts. "What about what Jaku told me? It's secondhand, too. Will it help?"

"Possibly." Jet didn't elaborate.

Too intimidated to pursue this line of questioning, I said, "Lots of us are scared with Jaku on the loose."

Jet crossed his arms over his chest. "What are you doing to protect yourself?"

"Getting an unlisted phone number and a post office box when I move in two days."

Jet nodded. "That's good. Take precautions."

Disappointed, I looked down, trying to hide my tears. Since Jet refused to question the panties at the fire department, I felt sure I would be the only one to testify against Jaku. I clutched my purse, wanting to run down the hall, away from this disdainful detective. Instead, I forced myself to say, "Thanks," and squelched the, "for nothing" wanting to squeeze through my lips.

Jet was saying something about fear but I shut him out, hearing only my own frightened thoughts. Later, I wondered if he was trying to prepare me for the way the defense attorney would interrogate me when he got me on the stand.

Outside the police building, the bright sunshine seared my bloodshot eyes. I pulled on sunglasses to defend against the glare, and wished I could defend against my sadness as easily. I hurried toward the anonymity of my car and quickly drove away.

As I entered my apartment, the phone rang. I almost didn't answer but decided I wasn't going to let Jaku scare me out of answering my own phone. Happily, it was Mom, calling to ask how the packing was going and if I'd been able to find enough boxes. Her kind tone of voice was balm to me after Jet's diatribe.

I told her about the boxes Vic had guided me to across the street, and how I'd sensed Vic's presence by the tingling in my head and the way the wind picked up until it practically blew me across the street. "It was the eeriest thing, Mom. One of the boxes had Liz written in big black letters on it. That box literally had my name on it! And I had this sweet feeling, like the air around me was charged with joy. I knew Vic was there."

Mom said, "Oh, really?" and "I see, dear," but I detected skepticism in her voice. After our conversation ended, I felt deflated. A few minutes later, the phone rang again. With some trepidation, I answered.

My mother's voice quivered with excitement. "The most amazing thing just happened, Liz! As soon as I hung up after talking to you, I heard a crash coming from the garage. I ran there and noticed a strong wind had knocked the top two cardboard boxes off a tall stack of boxes. This surprised me, because the stack has been there a long time, and the boxes are well-balanced. I went to pick them up and I saw both boxes had Liz written on the side. Those are the only two boxes I have of yours. It's a good omen. You're very powerful."

"Not me, Mom. I have a powerful spirit friend, and he can do things with boxes, and the wind, and electric lights."

"I believe you, dear," my mother said in her soothing way. "But let's not tell your father."

* * *

The next day, after my Saturday day shift, I drove back to my apartment. Squeezing past high stacks of cardboard boxes in my tiny living room, I stuffed pajamas into an overnight bag. I had said yes to an invitation from dad's friends, Mark and Phan Hamilton, to sleep over at their home. The phone rang. My "hello" was answered only by the click of a receiver and a dial tone.

I told myself I wouldn't let Jaku spook me, but I shook like a palm frond in a blustering wind. A few moments later, I locked the front door, scanned the neighborhood, and ran down the stairs. Inside the blue, womb-like interior of my VW bug, I relaxed. Two glorious weeks of leave awaited me, tomorrow was moving day, and I was driving somewhere Jaku couldn't find me.

Twilight gave way to night as I inched my way through sluggish traffic toward Haleiwa Town on the north shore. An hour later, Mark greeted me at the front door of his white brick home, martini in hand, his bushy white hair disheveled in the hands of a small boy whose legs straddled the old man's neck. He ushered me inside to meet another son and his thirty-something Vietnamese wife, Phan.

"Welcome to our home, Liz!" Phan's voice was warm and lilting. She patted an overstuffed pillow on the couch beside her. "I go put boys to bed now, please relax."

I sipped the wine cooler Mark handed me until she returned. The three of us talked long into the night about Vic, Jaku, and me. "Well, my dear, I can certainly see why you'd be scared," Mark said, finishing his third martini. "But you're completely safe here, so don't worry. Now I must get some sleep, but you and Phan can stay up as late as you like." He walked unsteadily away.

Phan moved closer to me on the couch. "Why do you think this man, this murderer, is the one call you up?"

"Because I feel it in my gut." I tucked a leg underneath me and turned to face her. "And because his phone calls started the day after Jaku was released from prison. My guess is he's calling to find out if I'm home."

"Heart know things head don't know." Phan unplaited the thick black braid hanging to her waist, and stared at me with large black eyes. "I know fortuneteller, her name Chan. I know her since I small girl in Hanoi when I live Vietnam. She very good. Many years ago, before I know Mark, she read for me. She say I will meet man older than me, rich man I be very compatible with."

Phan's hair rippled free, red highlights shining. "She tell me I marry him and have family life, have children fathered by him. I laugh at her. I one wild girl in those days, have plenty boyfriends. But Chan tell me true. Tell me lot more things. Most come true."

"Does the fortuneteller live on Oahu?"

Phan nodded and ran a wide-toothed comb through her thick mane. "If you like, I take you see her. She deal out cards, make you pick, tell you what mean. She tell you plenty things—about bad man, about good man, other things too. I like go again and dearly love take you. I think you believer. When you believe, she read for you easy."

I told her getting a reading from Chan would be great but, with my mother flying in the next day to help me set up my new place, I had to put it off for a few weeks.

She brought a tray with steaming cups of chamomile tea, packets of honey, and fortune cookies, and set it on the coffee table beside us. "When Mrs. Hartz go back mainland, we go see Chan."

"I can hardly wait." I pulled the small strip of paper from my fortune cookie and read, "The truth shall set you free."

* * *

Sunday was far from a day of rest for me or the guys helping me move. Deputy Chief Bob whistled as he walked through my new condo's spacious living room and bedroom, admiring the white concrete walls, plush beige carpet, and two red patios.

"This place is built like a fortress," he said, studying the burglar alarm control box and gesturing toward the alarm bells bolted to the patio roof outside the living room.

I nodded, pointing at locks on the sliding glass door tracks. "If anybody tries to break in, the alarm bells will wake up the whole neighborhood. And if those wires threaded through the sliding door screens are cut, the alarm will be set off, too."

"Cool your pad's secure," a fireman said, "and twice as big as the old one."

"Yes. Now I've got room for guests." I smiled. "Good thing, since I'm picking up my mom at the airport tonight."

Already dripping sweat from moving and arranging my stuff, the guys restacked boxes to give me sufficient space to spread out my futon in the living room. They also assembled my twin bed in the bedroom for my mom, hooked up the stereo, and put on a Chuck Mangione album I'd inherited from Vic.

"You guys are the best!" I announced. "Ready for pizza?"

"Yep." Joe lifted two steaming pizzas out of the oven and shoved two more inside.

"Where's the beer?" Tom yelled.

My answer, "In a cooler in my car," was met with applause.

Bob walked me to my parking stall, making note of how well-hidden it was from the street behind my condo.

"A plus," I told him.

"If you're ever scared, Mandy's and my home is yours," Bob said.

"Thanks." We lugged the heavy cooler inside. "My only worry is Jaku sending someone to follow me home from work. At least for the next two weeks, he can't."

Several hours later, the firemen bustled off with many thanks for the beer and pizza. After they left, I chased the silence away with a Rolling Stones album, and busied myself with unpacking, lining kitchen shelves with contact paper, arranging pots and pans, dishes, utensils and linens inside cabinets and drawers, and cleaning up.

I drove to the airport in the dark. Soon my mother's gentle voice saying, "Sweet dreams, honey," floated from the bedroom and spread like balm across my tired mind.

"You too, Mom." Lying on my futon, I pulled back the beige living room curtains and breathed in the cool air drifting through the screen doors. The sweet scent of mock orange blossoms wafted into the dark room. At the sight of the star-studded sky and the sound of leaves rustling on paper bark eucalyptus trees, I sighed. *Safe at last in my very own place.*

* * *

By the time another Sunday rolled around, I'd christened my energetic, white-haired, slim mother "The White Tornado," a name she poo-pooed but liked, judging by the way the corners of her mouth turned up slightly. With her at the helm, we unpacked everything and set up bookshelves, arranging my numerous books by title and subject.

Whisking me off to garage sales and department stores, she helped me select chairs and pillows and baskets that fit well with my bargain basement furniture. We brought our treasures home where she transformed my condo into a color-coordinated, homey space. I thanked her for performing miracles.

On Sunday night, to celebrate our accomplishments, we accepted an invitation from the Hamiltons for a home-cooked Vietnamese dinner. After I had dipped my seventh egg roll into a tasty sweet and sour sauce, Mom remarked, "I'm amazed my svelte daughter can eat so many eggrolls."

I licked my lips. "They're so delicious I could eat a dozen."

Phan spread her hands far apart to indicate platter after platter of aromatic food crowded together in bright bowls along the center of her dining room table. "Plenty egg rolls left. How you doing now, Liz? Not scared anymore?"

"Could I eat like this if I were?"

My words tickled Mark, who chuckled between sips of his martini. I added, "At least stark terror beats the heck out of dieting. I probably gained back the five pounds I lost in the last few weeks tonight, thanks to your great cooking."

Phan laughed. "Liz and I going shopping downtown in Chinatown in few weeks, Mrs. Hartz. I show her where to buy all ingredients for this kind food, for cheap."

Mom smiled politely. She knew I didn't do much fancy cooking.

"Phan promised to give me cooking lessons," I told my mother. "She's also going to take me to a fortune teller."

"Yes," Phan said. "Fortune teller very good."

"That should prove interesting," my mother said. "You'll have to tell me, Liz, what the fortune teller gleans from the cards for you."

* * *

For years I had scribbled my dreams on whatever was handy—sometimes in notebooks, more often on scraps of paper—believing dreams symbolized what went on in the hidden layers of my mind. Immediately upon waking, before wraithlike dream images dissolved, I grabbed the closest piece of paper and described the dream landscape with as much detail as I could muster, dated it, and shoved it into a box or folder.

On the morning after Phan's delicious dinner, I propped my back against a cold concrete living room wall and sorted through papers. Hundreds of loose-leaf pages of dreams were mixed in with business records and receipts, and scraps of poems and creative writings.

"You'll find developing a filing system and labeling each folder makes life easier when tax time rolls around," Mom said. She wrote "Bills-paid" on the tab of a manila folder.

"I'll do it." I stacked the papers spread across my lap into separate piles: business, creative writing, and dreams.

My mother sat on a folding chair in the middle of a jumble of papers scattered on top of carpet and boxes. "From here on out, you'll want to itemize your deductions. You'll be able to claim expenses—medical costs, mortgage interest, property taxes. Have you finished going through the papers in your file box?"

"Not yet. Everything's mixed in together, including writing excerpts and dreams I scribbled on scraps of paper. Some of my dreams are organized chronologically, but most are just shoved in this folder. Since they're dated, guess I should put them in order, too."

"Good idea, but for now I suggest you just separate them from your business records." Mom, always the gentle diplomat, gazed at me over her reading glasses. "I put my dreams in order," she added. "That way, I can figure out what my dream symbols mean and see a pattern. I keep a notebook on my bed table and date each entry."

"Sounds like a good plan, Mom. I'll switch to a dream notebook, too, and quit writing on scraps of paper."

I continued to thumb through papers until a dream, written in red ink on lined yellow paper, caught my eye. I had forgotten about it. I picked up the paper, read it, and reread it. I gasped. My heart beat more quickly.

"Wow! Mom! Listen to this one. I dreamed it on August 13 last year, on the Monday night Billy moved to Maui."

Mom raised an eyebrow. "Go ahead and read it to me, honey. But then let's get back to work."

I sat up straighter. Holding the sheet of paper with both hands, I read:

> *August 13, 1984. This dream was in vivid color.*
>
> *I dreamed Jaku kicked open the warped wooden front door of my Ward Avenue apartment. I had forgotten to lock the door, something I never forget in real life.*
>
> *He forced his way into bed with me. He wore a silver coin on a silver chain around his neck, just like he does at the fire station. He was halfway under the covers, and I had pulled the covers up to my neck. He kept touching me and saying, 'See? It's just touch, nothing wrong with touch.'*
>
> *I kept saying, 'No, no, no! Stop it, I don't want to.'*
>
> *The scene faded out, just like in the movies . . .*

I paused, breathed slowly and deeply, but failed to slow my staccato heartbeat. My hands shook as I resumed:

> *. . . and then faded in to the living room. I stood there in my bathrobe and Jaku was joking and laughing. I was afraid people wouldn't understand, would think I had invited him in.*

All of a sudden, this huge, muscular man's arm came through the window from outside and grabbed me on the shoulder. His touch was warm and reassuring, and filled me with complete and utter joy. I knew, whoever that muscular arm belonged to, he understood I had not, would never have, invited Jaku in.

I swallowed hard and added, "After I wrote the dream down I scribbled these notes:

I think that arm belongs to Billy and the dream's telling me he'll come back and work things out with me. Billy knows Jaku's a punk. He must want to protect me from him.

I whispered, "That's it."

"Good heavens, Liz, what a frightening dream!" Mom frowned. "Why, you're as white as a ghost." She sat beside me on the carpet and wrapped a warm arm around my shoulders. "But it's nothing to get upset about."

"Mom." I felt faint. "All of a sudden, reading this dream, I understand things I didn't understand before. It means more than what I wrote down. I don't think this is a run-of-the-mill, symbolic-type dream."

My mother's frown deepened. "Well, what then?"

"It's the answer to a prayer, only I dreamed it six months before I said the prayer." I struggled to find words to explain. "See, on Valentine's Day, after Tony and I ran to Jaku's apartment and found out he'd killed Vic, I hurried home and prayed to God to send me a dream that would tell me what the argument was about."

I wiped my damp forehead with the back of my hand and continued, "I didn't get an answer that day, or later. I got the answer six months before, in this dream I dreamed on the night Billy left me."

"Maybe you're right, and maybe you're not." Mom shrugged. "Some dreams don't mean anything more than the steak you had for dinner upset your stomach."

"True, Mom." I felt faint. "But this one meant Jaku was planning to . . . to . . . attack me. He told Vic about his plans, maybe invited him to join in the fun because he thought Vic was like him, since they'd had a drunken threesome once. But Vic was never like him. Jaku didn't know how close Vic and I had become during those last six weeks when Jaku was on leave." The implications of the dream ricocheted through me. "They were arguing—"

Mom interrupted, "Now don't go jumping to conclusions."

I grabbed her arm. "Don't you see? Vic Lazzarini died protecting me!"

"You don't know that," she insisted.

"That's why I still feel him around me." The pieces of the Vic/Jaku puzzle finally fit seamlessly together for me.

"Liz, I think you're reading entirely too much into a dream which could have any number of meanings." Mom's lower lip trembled. "And please don't go feeling like you're responsible for your friend's death, because you're not. Whatever the argument was about, you didn't know anything about it."

Mom's arm still circled my shoulders. I felt her worry wrap around me, too. Why was I upsetting my mother? Not wanting her to stress out on my account, I said, "You're right. Guess I got carried away. The dream could mean a lot of things. And I don't feel guilty. Like you said, I didn't know what was going on between Vic and Jaku. So don't worry." I squeezed her arm. "Thanks for calming me down. You know me, the high drama queen."

Mom smiled. We went back to sorting. Well, I tried to sort, but I couldn't keep my mind on the papers in front of me. Everything fell into place like cascading dominoes. The reason I still felt Vic around me was he had a message for me, that his last words and thoughts were about me. The reason Jaku kept calling was because he wanted me to back up his story, to say Vic had been making obscene phone calls to me instead of the other way around. The reason I had the dream the night Billy left was because it was showing me that, the moment I started living alone, I became a potential victim in Jaku's mind.

Later, while my mother slept in the bedroom, I sat cross-legged on my futon and wrote in my journal, "I'm totally awestruck to have had a friend like Vic."

I stared past the yellow popcorn orchids lining the edge of my red patio, gazed at the bright full moon in the ebony sky, watched monkey pod tree branches sway in the stiff breeze, and felt as if living waters flowed through me.

Words I remembered from the Bible seemed to describe what I'd experienced exactly. Matthew 6.8: *For your Father knows the things you have need of before you ask Him.* John 15.13: *There is no greater love than this; that a man lay down his life for his friends.*

I thought about Vic losing his life protecting mine. I thought about the dream I dreamed six months before Jaku murdered Vic, and how God revealed what would happen long before it did. I thought about the man I feared and the man I loved having an argument about me, and how their battle jumped inside of me and became my struggle between fear and conscience. I thought about God allowing me to discover what Vic and Jaku were arguing about only after I felt the fear and told the truth anyway.

My worry about testifying against Jaku dissolved. My determination to see him convicted intensified. "I will do everything in my power to ensure Jaku is locked up in prison where he belongs," I said softly to a color torso snapshot of Vic wearing a black denim jacket, scotch-taped to the wall beside his shell chandelier. Moonlight shining through the sliding glass doors reflected in Vic's deep blue eyes.

"And I'll hone my writing skills until I can describe what happened so compellingly readers will clamor to read your story. So the whole wide world will know what a righteous dude you were, and that your spirit transcended the grave, and that a dream solved the mystery of what the argument was about. I promise to get you in print, Vic, or die trying."

Chapter 8

Thursday, March 28, through Monday, April 22

A COOL BREEZE ruffled the beige curtains in my living room. Loudly flapping wings heralded the descent of a congregation of birds onto a monkey pod tree across the street, where they raucously serenaded the dawn.

My mother's rhythmic breathing in the bedroom harmonized with the cadence of crickets in the dewy grass outside my patio. I tiptoed to the dining table and wrote in my journal: "Should I tell Jet about the dream?"

I couldn't see myself sitting in a cold cubicle in Homicide, looking at Jet's stern face and saying, "I know Vic died protecting me. How? I had this precognitive dream, and I often feel the presence of his spirit. Why? I think he still wants to protect me."

I wrote, "I think I owe it to Vic to tell Jet my truth."

Should I phone Jet instead? No, the idea of calling him and talking about something so far beyond the physical facts made me cringe.

I wrote, "Worst case scenario, Jet will think me even wackier than he already does. Best case, he'll hear me."

Should I write Jet a letter? I imagined he would come down on me hard if I wrote him about my dream and Vic's spirit presence. I could almost hear his indignant voice on the phone saying, "What do you take me for? Precognitive dreams, spirits hovering?" Then he would hiss, "I'm a professional!" and slam the phone down.

My face flushed at the thought. But writing Jet seemed like my best option, as long as I kept my words ambiguous so he wouldn't immediately discredit them.

Two days later, and minutes after my mother and I said our tearful goodbyes at the airport, I mailed a letter to Jet. I'd written I wanted to talk to him about something that would shed light on what Jaku and Vic were arguing about, and asked him if I could talk to him in person, somewhere away from the police station.

I included my phone number and added, if I didn't hear from him, I would take it as a refusal to meet and talk. I wrote my return address on the envelope so Jet could tell the police to keep a watchful eye on me if he thought I might still be in danger from Jaku.

* * *

I hoped that April Fools' Day was not a bad day to consult a psychic. "Fortune teller, she about eighty percent accurate on future," Phan said. We walked through a dry, weedy yard surrounding a peeling green house. "But she hundred percent when tell the past and present." Phan knocked on the front door.

"I can hardly wait." I hoped she'd be every bit as accurate as Phan thought she was.

A thin little girl with enormous black eyes and straight-as-a-string black hair opened the door. The child silently stared at me and hugged Phan's knees.

A large dining room table surrounded by torn vinyl kitchen chairs occupied the middle of the room. Long, worn couches lined two walls, and a sink, stove and refrigerator lined another. Three young girls with round faces and straight black hair sprawled across one of the battered couches, playing games and speaking Vietnamese until they saw me, whereupon they stopped talking and fixed me with silent stares. A baby boy slept on a comforter on the other couch.

Phan introduced me to Chan, a petite, pretty woman with a clear, rosy complexion, round face, and big, black eyes. "And this Sally. She translator," Phan said, nodding at a thin woman with curly black hair who sat kitty-cornered from Chan at the kitchen table. "Chan English not too good," Phan explained.

The littlest girl started to cry, and screamed something unintelligible at her sisters. "I take children to park so Chan can concentrate," Phan said. She gathered up the girls and left.

Chan smiled and motioned me over to the chair beside her. She placed a deck of cards on the table in front of me. In halting English, she told me to cut them three times. Next she had me pick seven cards from the deck, which she laid out on the table, face up, in a row. After dealing out several rows of cards, face down, she said something to Sally in Vietnamese.

"Chan say easy to read for you because you believer," Sally translated.

I nodded.

"You have roommate," Chan said.

I shook my head. "I live alone."

Chan looked startled, then spoke to Sally again in Vietnamese.

"She says her guides say you have roommate," Sally said. "Strong energy around you. Someone stay with you."

"I live alone," I repeated. Darn, I had hoped she'd be more perceptive.

"You talk to judge. In courtroom," Chan spoke slowly in careful English. "Time long past. When teenager."

"Yes. I had to testify against a shoplifter when I worked as a sales clerk at Montgomery Ward. Long ago. I was a senior in high school." My heartbeat quickened.

"You two bad accidents," Chan continued, slowly. "First one, you twist left leg very bad. Other one, you hard time to raise right arm."

"Yes! When I was 16, my left leg got badly twisted when my ski came off as I skied down a steep slope. And in 1970, after receiving a whiplash when I was rear-ended by a car, I had trouble lifting my right arm." My heart pounded even faster.

She closed her eyes for a long moment before repeating, "You have roommate. He not of this world. He stay around you."

A tingling sensation electrified my spine. "Who is this . . . spirit?" I asked.

She smiled. "You know who he. He man you love. Very mean man murder him."

Amazing. "What else do you see about the murder?"

She leaned toward me, her eyes black luminescent pools. "Man you love, he very good man. Love you very much, have great respect for you. Other man, he very mean man. Very angry. He want to kill your sweetheart dead, dead, dead."

"What was the argument about?" I asked. "Was it work related?"

Chan gave Sally a puzzled look, and the two of them spoke briefly in Vietnamese. Then they pulled their chairs closer and leaned toward me. The sympathetic aura emanating from these two women warmed and comforted me.

"Not work-related," Chan said. "Argument about you. Man who dead—what name?"

"Vic," I whispered. "Vic Lazzarini."

"Vic tell mean man, 'You leave her alone. She mine, I love her, I want marry her, and you getting in way.'"

Vic wanted to marry me? Could this really be true? The blood seemed to rush from my head. I felt faint, and gripped the table edge tightly, as if holding onto something physical would also help me hold onto consciousness. "Can you tell me what the murderer was saying?" I whispered.

Chan touched my arm, her hand as hot as fire. Her touch steadied and energized me. She must have intuited this, for a smile flickered across her face before she frowned and said, "Mean man, bad plans for you. He want harm you. Vic, his spirit protect you. You have roommate. You feel him, no?"

"Yes." I pressed my right hand against my shoulder. "I often feel him this close."

"Vic spirit protect you," Chan repeated.

"Will anybody murder the murderer?" I asked.

She dashed my hopes with a shake of her head. "Nobody bother him. He very mean man." She dealt out several more cards and spoke to Sally in Vietnamese.

Sally nodded. "Chan say do not talk at trial."

"But I told the police everything. They might make me testify against Jaku."

Chan dealt out three more cards on the table and studied them for a few moments. "You be very careful," Chan said haltingly. "If talk at trial about bad man, after things die down, he send someone after you. If talk, he try for murder you."

I stuttered. "Can . . . can you tell me more about this?"

"Someone try catch ride with you at night. Do not pick up. If you careful, you be all right. Nothing going happen to you." Chan smiled. "I like you. Nothing bad happen to you." She studied the cards again. "Mean man be free 'til trial. Maybe get off. Have good lawyer."

I chewed on that possibility while Chan dealt out five more cards, studied them and said, "Next year you married. Have two children, boy and girl. Be very happy. How old you now?"

"Thirty-four."

"Not look like!" she exclaimed.

I felt flattered, but wondered if the having-kids prediction was her stock line to unmarried women, most of whom longed to be wives and mothers.

"In two years, be happiest year of your life. You be very happy. You be like me, fortune teller. Very good, you help people."

"Can you tell me anything about my future husband?" I asked.

"Him very good with computers. Will love you very much. Will take good care of you. But you be careful. Vic, he still love you. Not want you marry. Not want you live long life. Want you go with him."

Still stunned by the idea of Vic wanting to marry me, I hoped he could hear my thought, *I want to be with you, too, Vic. If I could will myself by your side, I would.*

Chan asked, "No more questions?"

"Do you have any other advice for me?"

Chan closed her eyes for a long moment. When she opened them, her expression was wistful. "You must wait. Be patient. This not going be good year for you. Not easy time. You cry, cry, cry, miss man you love." The touch of her small, plump hand on my cold ones reassured me. "Next year better. But now, have to cry. Understand?"

I nodded, tears spilling down my cheeks. Remembering what Phan had said to do when the reading was finished, I pressed a twenty-dollar bill into her hand.

"I like you." Chan squeezed my hand. "You very good."

"Thank you," I squeezed her back, "for your words of wisdom."

Phan breezed in with a flurry of little girls, and handed them over to the translator, who took the children outside. I sat on the couch, trying to read a magazine I'd brought with me while Chan and Phan chattered in Vietnamese.

After Phan's reading, she drove me home, saying she'd be back in an hour to take me shopping in Chinatown. Dizzy with the implications of Chan's words, I welcomed the time alone.

I leaned against the kitchen counter and gazed at the large living room Vic would never share with me. His white shell chandelier gleamed in the sunlight above my round wooden table. His porthole-shaped aquarium, home to two bright blue beta fish, hung from the ceiling in the corner closest to my patio door. His albums and reel-to-reel tapes stacked in blue plastic packing crates rested against the west wall.

"Vic," I announced to the empty room, "you're the man I love, you're my knight in armor, you're my hero forever. I sit beneath your chandelier, and play your music, and think about you."

When Phan returned, I told her, "I'd give anything to know which twenty percent of Chan's future predictions are wrong."

Phan's laughter sounded like tinkling bells. "Only time tell you that."

* * *

Two nights later, Whaler Fire Department's sole male alarm room operator greeted me with a toothy grin. "Hard to come back to work after two weeks leave, sí?"

"Sí, especially to a midnight shift." I yawned. "Anything happening, amigo?"

"No, señorita," he shook his balding head. "Same old shit."

After he left, I changed the recording tapes, typed recaps of the day's fire responses, skimmed the pass-on log, and settled into a pulp-fiction thriller I hoped would keep me awake. Half an hour later, a business phone line rang.

"Whaler Fire Department. Liz speaking." A long pause at the other end preceded the click of the receiver hanging up.

It starts again. My jaw muscles tensed at the thought that Jaku, who should have been behind bars, still walked the streets, free to cause me harm.

Well, I wasn't going to let him, but I had to remain vigilant. When my shift ended, I drove home by way of the back gate in case Jaku's thugs lurked outside the main gate, intent on following me home.

* * *

Three days later, I watched through the alarm room large window as lightning sliced jagged silver pathways through the black sky and illuminated panels of rain blowing sideways. The taxiway turned into a river, blown by swift trade winds past the open bay garage.

The phone panel reminded me of blinking Christmas tree lights. By 1 a.m., I had already dispatched fire trucks twice to downed electrical power lines and sent five crews of emergency plumbers and electricians to flooding in base housing.

"I haven't been so busy since Hurricane Iwa," I told Jim, a fire captain who was helping me answer phone calls from callers reporting flooded quarters.

The direct line from Base Operations rang. "Hey, Fire Department, I don't like to bother you, busy as you must be, but maintenance says all taxiway lights on Runway Six Right went out. We need them fixed ASAP."

I groaned. The electricians were already working on downed power lines and a blown transformer. Now I would have to call every guy in the shop until one of them deigned to answer the phone. "I'll get somebody out there. Might take a while, though."

I wished I could dispatch Vic. He had recently taken to playing with the overhead light in the adjoining assistant chief's office. First his presence would announce itself by a tingling sensation in my head. Then the light would blink on and off.

No sooner had the thought, *I'll bet Vic flicks the lights just to play,* popped into my mind than I felt the familiar psychic sensations, and the lights flicked off and on.

"Vic did that," I said.

Jim shook his head. "Don't talk to me about no ghosts."

The Base Ops phone rang again. "Hey, Fire Department!" the man sounded excited. "Maintenance just called again. They said the lights came back on. All by themselves! Hey, how'd you do that?"

I smiled. "I have powerful friends in high places."

"You scare me," he said and hung up.

I laughed and silently thanked Vic. How did he do it? Electricity was energy, and he was an energy being now so maybe he could merge with the current or affect it or . . . I rolled possibilities around in my mind.

"What's so funny?" Jim asked.

I swiveled in my chair to face him. "The guy at Base Ops thinks I magically fixed the lights on the taxiway." Jim smiled a conspiratorial grin until I added, "He doesn't know Vic did it. Vic can make the lights go on and off. Don't ask me how."

Jim stared at me with a you-are-a-space-case look. "I don't know about you."

How could I explain it to Jim? You really had to feel Vic's presence to understand.

* * *

Thirty-six hours later, cotton candy clouds blew across an early morning sky the color of Vic's deep blue eyes. The warm sunshine and moist trade winds persuaded me to set the security alarm and lock the door behind me. Although I doubted Jaku had found out where I lived, I would keep to the back streets, counting on caution to keep me safe in case I had to testify against him.

A few miles from my condo, a neighborhood park beckoned. I wanted to squish the cool green grass between my toes as I walked barefoot past paper-bark trees and red hibiscus bushes. I wanted to watch children laughing and swinging and skidding down slides, and remember how it felt to be free.

I donned a floppy hat and was walking briskly past picnic tables when the wind swept up dry leaves and swirled them on the ground around my feet. I stood still, a willing captive of the red, brown and golden circling leaves. A change of temperature, the wind cooler now, combined with a characteristic tingling in my head, had me thinking, *Nice day for a walk, Vic. The dancing leaves are lovely.*

My hat blew off and raced down the sidewalk in front of me. I ran after it, laughing as it swirled away each time I reached for it. Finally, I snatched it and tied it securely under my chin. *Vic, you're such a tease!* The thrill of Vic's presence pushed thoughts of Jaku away.

That night, I dreamed I was learning how to fly off a pier, and Vic was coaching me on how to avoid a crash landing. The connection with Vic was so deep and strong, it seemed as though we breathed together.

"You're doing good," he said. Placing his left hand on his chest and touching his right hand to the hot skin above my fluttering heart, he added, "We're beating in perfect sync."

I pressed my small, thin hands into his large ones. His body grew taller, his hair darkening, and somehow I knew he was altering his image so I would see him as the tall, dark, and handsome Prince Charming of my fantasies. *No need to change your appearance, Vic. You're already the man of my dreams.*

My dream reflection in the jalousie window of his studio apartment showed me wearing a flowing white wedding dress. "Oh," he said, "I guess I should carry you over the threshold," and he reached down and lifted me off my feet.

I wrapped my arms around his neck. We kissed a long, slow, sweet kiss. My heart warmed and opened wide and a river of ecstasy flowed through me, like a waterfall, like rapids, like electricity plugging me into life. I felt totally accepted, like I absolutely belonged, like my every cell was cherished. Never had I imagined love could make me feel so alive.

At dawn, as the mundane world's physical outline started to form in my still blissed-out mind, I tried to go back to sleep so I could remain in the warm circle of Vic's arms. But by the time the golden sky turned to blue my joy was already fading.

* * *

On the following Sunday, the station buzzed with speculation about what Jaku was up to. After dinner, Jim told me two firemen from Whaler, Greg and Morry, had run into Jaku at Waikiki Beach on the previous day. "The way Morry told it, Jaku knew about everything going on in the station. Jaku and Greg seemed real buddy-buddy."

I rolled my chair closer to Jim. "Did Jaku say anything about the argument?"

Jim nodded.

"Jaku claimed Vic had been making obscene phone calls to you, and Jaku was threatening to turn Vic in to the chief. This enraged Vic, who charged at Jaku with a gun." Jim grimaced. "But Jaku, being the street-smart dude he is, was packing a concealed gun, and shot Vic before Vic could shoot him."

"Old quick draw, huh?" I snorted. "The part about the concealed gun is probably the only true thing Jaku said. Vic would never have stood there arguing if Jaku had been waving a gun in his face."

Jim frowned. "Morry said Jaku made him sick the way he talked about Vic being six feet under, may he rest in peace. So sarcastic, like he was joking about it."

"I wonder if, now and then, Jaku regrets shooting the best friend he ever had," I said.

Jim said, "I doubt it," and added that Greg brayed like a donkey at the things Jaku said. "Greg's probably the reason Jaku knows everything going on in the station," he said.

"Oh, no!" Maybe Greg's mouth was catapulting me into danger.

Jim raised an eyebrow. "Say what?"

"What if one of the firemen from the other shift, somebody who helped me move, tells Greg where I live now? Do you think Greg would tell Jaku?"

Jim gave me a condescendingly smile. "The two shifts don't interact much. I wouldn't worry about it."

I decided Jim was right. I shouldn't worry. Instead, I would act. I would talk to the guys who helped me move, and swear them to secrecy. And I would come up with a convincing lie for Greg.

On Tuesday, April 9, I stopped by Carey's house before my 4 o'clock swing shift began. She poured me a cup of tea, and asked, "Kind of unbelievable, isn't it, Vic saying he wanted to marry you, when he didn't even kiss you on your double date?"

I spooned honey into my steaming cup. "Even so, I think Chan was right."

"Why?"

"Because of what Jaku told the security police when he came on base. First, let me backtrack. Remember when I told you Jaku switched the story around when he told Jet Vic was making obscene phone calls to me, and that's what the argument was about?"

Carey nodded. "So what did Jaku tell the S.P.s?"

"He told them that he, Jaku, was planning to marry some girl, and Vic was getting in the way." A lump formed in my throat.

Carey spilled tea on the plastic tablecloth. "I get it. Jaku switched the story again."

"Right. Phan told me the fortune teller's 100 percent accurate when she looks into the past." The hot tea soothed my tight throat. "In light of what Jaku told the cops, Chan must be right about what Vic was saying to Jaku that morning. Vic loved me and I didn't even know it." I thought about Vic carrying me over the threshold in my dream. A tear plopped into my teacup.

"Well, how could you know? He never told you, did he?"

"No." I blew my nose. "But I knew he was shy. And I knew he liked me."

"'Like's not love, and it was up to him to tell you." Carey opened her mouth to say more but a wail from the nursery distracted her. "Peggy's awake. Excuse me."

She disappeared down the hallway, leaving me with my thoughts about what might have been. I didn't realize sadness showed on my face until Carey stood beside me, Peggy straddling her hip, and said, "Are you okay?"

"I've been better." Peggy stretched out her chubby little arms. I held her close. "But I'd be worse if I didn't have you to confide in."

Carey's smile was warmer than Peggy in my arms. "That's what friends are for."

* * *

On the following day, for the third time, I started to dial Homicide, and for the third time I stopped. I wanted to tell Jet about the suspicious phone calls, but nothing concrete tied them to Jaku. Would he think I was a hysterical female with a wild imagination? I finally forced my fingers to dial.

"Yamasato," Jet said.

"This is Liz Hartz. I think Jaku is after me because he blames me for breaking up his friendship with Vic," I blurted in one quick breath.

A pause followed before Jet said, "You shouldn't have written me that letter."

"Why not?" Nervousness made my voice shrill.

"You should have phoned, like you're doing now," he said softly.

His words left me tongue-tied. There was no way I could tell Jet about Vic's spirit presence and how he breezed in with the wind and made the lights blink, at least not over the phone.

Jet broke the silence. "But if this is what you wanted to talk about, you're assuming the argument was about you."

"But," I stammered, "my life may be in danger! I've been getting phone calls—"

He interrupted, his voice brusque. "If you're getting phone calls, tell the police."

Intimidated, I whispered, "Okay." Then I thought, *Aren't you the police?* But Jet had already hung up. *Okay, caustic cop. I'll find another Dick Tracy to talk to.*

Grabbing some notebook paper, I wrote by the light of the bulb dangling inside Vic's chandelier about the obscene phone call, and how a mysterious caller was phoning me at work and hanging up when I answered. I wrote: *I think it's Jaku. He must realize I told the police the truth about the obscene phone call that he, not Vic, made to me.*

I ended by saying my sole purpose in writing this letter was so the police would know who was responsible if something happened to me.

The closest police station was five miles away, in Wahiawa Town in Central Oahu. I drove there as fast as the law would allow. Inside the red-brick building, I spotted a door with the words "Criminal Investigation" imprinted on amber glass. When I pushed the door open, a man with black hair, a thick mustache, and olive skin looked at me from behind a large oak desk. His brass name plate read: "Detective William Cabral."

"What can I do for you, ma'am?" Cabral's mouth smiled but his eyes did not.

I held out my statement to him. "My life may be in danger."

With a startled expression, Cabral shot up from his chair, grabbed the paper from my hand, and gestured toward an overstuffed chair. "Sit down, ma'am! Take a load off."

I sank into the soft chair. His eyes scanned the paper, and he dragged his chair close to mine. "Who's the detective in charge of this case?" he asked.

"Jet Yamasato."

"Did you tell Jet about this?"

"Yes. I called him earlier today."

"What did he say?" Cabral's brown eyes studied my face.

"'You're assuming the argument was about you.' And also, 'If you're getting phone calls, tell the police.'" I shrugged. "So I'm telling you."

Cabral leaned closer. "Don't worry. I'll make sure Jet gets this."

"Thanks."

He walked me to the door. "Where do you live?"

"Just off Leilani Drive, in the Terrace Apartments, a few miles from here."

He held the door open for me. "Have you ever seen anyone who looked suspicious hanging around your place?"

"No. And Jaku doesn't know where I live. Only a few close friends know. And I have an unlisted phone number."

"If you ever see strangers hanging around your place, phone the police." Cabral frowned. "The police will definitely respond for this."

"It's unlikely he can find out where I live unless he sends some of his thug friends to follow me home." I couldn't stop my voice from shaking. "When I get those phone calls at work, I drive home by way of the back gate. But I worry Jaku will figure out what I'm doing."

A few days later, I was watering the aloe plants crowding my red lanai's concrete floor when Norma, the grandmotherly woman from Vic's apartment building, phoned. She told me Vic's sister Betty had phoned and said she'd received two threatening phone calls.

"The first caller said, 'Vic no stay dead. I seen him riding in a car beside Jaku with my own two eyes.' Betty starts crying. Then the low-life tells her she'd better not make trouble for Jaku. Or else. A few minutes later, the second caller phones. He says, 'No way brudduh Jaku gonna rot in jail. If he go prison, you gonna pay.'"

"Poor Betty, to be subjected to this." I wondered if the first caller had seen Vic's ghost.

"My lands, yes. That little worm is still up to no good, bothering her like this. And stupid! As if she has anything to do with whether or not he goes to prison."

"Wait a minute, Norma." I pictured the three newspaper articles about Vic's death. "Betty's name wasn't in the newspapers. Only Lola's name. The newspapers got it wrong, remember? They said Vic only had the one sister living in Michigan."

"Why, you're absolutely right. I have all the clippings. Not a word about Betty."

We decided Jaku must have sneaked through Vic's papers at his apartment and written down phone numbers, including Betty's. Norma said she would phone Betty back, and suggest she contact the detectives and tell them about the phone calls.

I stepped over water pooling in the grass and turned off the hose. *Good. When Jet hears about those phone calls to Betty, he'll know the ones I'm getting aren't just wrong numbers I'm panicking about.*

On the following day, I was back in the alarm room after dinner and had settled into a new chapter of a pulp fiction book when the red fire phone rang. "Whaler Fire Department," I said. "Are you reporting an emergency?"

"Can you help me?" whispered a woman with a local accent. "I need a friend for talk to. Can talk to me on another phone? One that doesn't record?"

My mind shifted into overdrive, questioning: "How does she know these phones record? Who told her I can talk on a non-recording phone a few steps away?" I tried to keep panic out of my voice. "You'll have to call back on 726-6385, the business line, ma'am. Then I'll pick up the line in the next office, and it won't record."

Her fervent "mahalo" before the phone went dead left me shaking and sure it was Jaku, not her, who wanted to talk to me without fear of being recorded. Part of me wanted to oblige, just to see what he'd say. Another part was afraid to talk if he knew I was not recording him; was afraid he would threaten me if I didn't tell the police what he wanted.

The business phone rang. The girl again. I said, "Just a minute. I'll switch to a phone that doesn't record."

I decided to try and trick the caller, so I put her line on hold and picked up a different line in the alarm room.

"Hello. This line doesn't record, ma'am," I said, thinking, *I've only got two minutes.* "How may I help you?"

Silence. Was Jaku's desperate intention to avoid prison forcing him to get me on the phone? Was he determined to coerce me no matter what the risk? If I spoke to him and he took offense at what I said, would he send his thugs after me?

"Is anyone there?" I asked.

Someone coughed and what sounded like a male voice whispered, "Please . . ."

My heart pounded wildly and I couldn't think straight. The beep of the recorder sounded. The caller slammed the receiver in my ear.

I wished I'd taken a chance and talked to him, wished even more I'd had a recording device to attach to the phone in the adjacent office so I could have recorded the caller incognito. After my heartbeat slowed, I phoned an inventor friend who knew everything there was to know about electronics and owed me a favor. I told him about Jaku and asked if I could call upon his electronic wizardry.

"My pappy always said paybacks were a bitch," he chuckled, "but not this time. I'm happy to help." He promised to throw something suitable together in the way of a recording device for me. We arranged to meet on the following morning.

Two days later, warm, moist wind caressed my skin when I stepped out of my VW in the Wahiawa Police Station parking lot. As before, the lobby felt freezer cold. Detective Cabral spotted me looking through the glass pane into his office and motioned me inside.

No sooner had the words, "I received another phone call" exited my mouth than my body started shaking.

He pulled a chair close to the desk for me. "Did you tell Jet?" he asked.

I sank into the chair. "I tried to but he wasn't in his office."

The detective said, "Tell me about the phone call."

I relayed the details. "When Jaku had the girl say, 'I need a friend,' I realized he still thinks I'm his friend."

Cabral squinted at me. "How you figure?"

"He doesn't know what I told the police. I always pretended to be his friend, to protect myself. Looks like I deceived the deceiver." I smiled, proud of myself.

"Don't be too sure."

My certainty instantly dissolved. "You're right," I whispered. "I can't be sure of anything."

"Maybe you're right and maybe you're not." Cabral shrugged. "Main thing you need to do now is take precautions."

I nodded. "I drove home by the back roads last night. If Jaku calls again and I record the conversation, can it be used as evidence against him?"

Cabral's emphatic "Yes!" was followed by the question, "Do you have a recording device?"

I nodded again. "A friend made me one. He gave it to me this morning."

"Did you test it? Does it work?"

"Yes and yes."

Cabral's eyes widened. He smiled. I continued, "If Jaku calls again, I'll record the conversation. I intend to lie to him and say I didn't tell the police anything."

"Yes! Say whatever you feel you need to say. After you finish your conversation and he hangs up, say your name, the time and date, and where this was recorded."

I promised to follow his instructions exactly.

"Do you still live in the Terrace Apartments a few miles from here?"

"Yes. In apartment B-103."

"You still haven't seen any strangers hanging around your condo, have you?"

"No."

As I drove home I imagined plain-clothes policemen staking out my apartment, keeping an eye on things. Now that he knew my address, I wondered if Cabral would have my place watched. I also wondered if I'd been reading too many detective novels.

Four days later, an oven fire in base housing kept me in the alarm room until almost time for the kitchen to close. The only food left simmering in the warming tray was some overcooked collard greens and greasy creamed chicken. I paid the cashier and noticed the dining area was empty except for Greg Kahala, a young airman who, according to the grapevine, still hung out with Jaku.

"Okay if I join you for dinner?" I asked.

Greg nodded and gestured toward an empty chair. I sank into it, my heart racing as I mentally rehearsed my speech.

"What's up, Liz?"

"Oh, lots of things. For one, I'm living on base now."

His eyebrows arched in surprise. "Nah! I thought you moved into a place up Wahiawa side."

Did he know where I lived? Had he told Jaku? I struggled to keep my voice steady, "I did. But my friend Carey asked me to stay on base with her to help with the kids while her husband's TDY. So I rented my condo out for a while."

"Nah! For real?"

"Yes. And guess what else? I just got a letter from Billy. He may get a job in Honolulu, and if he does, he's coming back for good." I hoped I looked happy.

"All right, Liz. Your old man coming back, eh? Cool."

"I'll know next week. I sure hope so."

After dinner, Deputy Chief Bob, seeing my pasty face as I stumbled back into the alarm room, asked, "What's wrong?"

"I'm shook up from lying to Greg." I sank into my chair. "The drawback is I'll have to tell everybody the same story. But it's worth it if Greg tells Jaku, and it stops him from sending someone to follow me home."

Bob chuckled. "Well, it certainly won't be the first time a false rumor has circulated through the station. I can't see as how it'll do any harm. And it may do you some good."

* * *

On the following night, I was reading on the couch in my condo when loudly flapping wings and shrill cries from birds descending on a yellow shower tree across the street beckoned me to my patio. The sweet scent of mock orange blossoms drifted past, and songbirds exuberantly sang their sundown songs. *Nice to have the night off from work. Wish Vic were here to share it with.*

Night came quickly. The Milky Way spread like a sequined ribbon across the cloudless sky. The sounds of wind rustling the leaves in the trees lining the sidewalk and the metallic tinkling of my wind chimes dangling from the patio roof lulled me to sleep.

I woke up to a loud "swoosh, swoosh, swoosh" sound. The clock's LED green letters read 1:30 a.m. "Swoosh, swoosh, swoosh" again. My curiosity turned to dread when I realized the sound was footsteps on the thick wet grass beyond my patio. I lay still, my heart wildly pounding, covers up to my neck. Too afraid to pull the curtains back and look out, I shook so hard the bed squeaked on its box springs. Had Jaku's henchmen finally found me?

Determined not to go down without a fight, I wobbled on rubber legs into the living room. Somehow my fingers managed to dial 911. Less than five minutes later, a loud knocking on my front door sent me scurrying to the peephole. I deactivated the alarm on the security panel, unbolted the front door, and flung it open.

Two large men in police uniforms faced me with holstered guns, their bright blue car flashers lighting up the parking lot. "The sound of someone walking in the grass stopped," I said, "but would you mind checking my patio for footprints? I was afraid to pull back the curtain. The patio's wet, so footprints would show, don't you think?"

The policemen looked at each other, then back at me. One of them said, "All right, ma'am."

They followed me to my bedroom. I unlocked the glass doors and pulled the curtains back. The green lawn behind my apartment sloped up to the street, beyond which ran another sidewalk, and beyond that, a high rise. No one was visible. One of the officers shone his flashlight onto the patio. "There are no footprints, ma'am. And there would be if someone had walked there, because the grass is wet from the rain."

"Well, I didn't actually hear someone on my patio." The two men glanced at each other again, and I hoped they didn't think I was a space cadet. "I just heard someone walking on the grass and was afraid it might be someone planning to break in."

"What did the noise sound like?" one of them asked.

"Swoosh, swoosh, swoosh." I wished I could mimic the sound more precisely.

"Swoosh, swoosh, swoosh?" the policemen asked in unison.

"Someone must have been walking on the grass," I repeated, feeling foolish. "The night's so still I heard the noise loud and clear. Maybe I'm a little nervous. I had some chairs and plants stolen off my patio last week." This was true, and easier than trying to explain my connection to a killer.

"Better safe than sorry," one of the officers said.

I walked them to the front door and thanked them for checking out the patio. "I was afraid to open the curtains and look out," I repeated. *Afraid Jaku's thugs might be standing there.*

"This place is built like a fortress," one of the officers remarked as they walked out the door. "That should make you feel a little more secure."

"It does. A little." An idea flashed and I asked, "Do you work at the Wahiawa Police Station?" They nodded. "Would you please let Detective Cabral know you came here tonight?" They just looked at me. "I talked to him recently about another matter, and he told me to call the police if any strangers showed up around my place."

One of them said, "We'll let him know, ma'am."

I thanked them for coming, locked the door behind them, reset my alarm and walked back to the bedroom. Plopping onto the bed, I gasped, "Swoosh, swoosh, swoosh!" and laughed hysterically. *I bet they think I'm a panty.*

My laughter subsided. *I guess I'm more stressed out than I realized. Why is this happening in my life? If Vic were still alive, he would have come over before now for a housewarming party. Like we planned.*

These thoughts brought tears and I was soon crying as hysterically as I'd been laughing a moment before. I hoped I wasn't cracking up. I just couldn't afford to go nuts, at least not until Jaku was behind bars, in case I had to help put him there.

Drained of all but fatigue, I turned off the lights. I had a hard time going back to sleep, and when I did, I dreamed of a fat-bellied man with a scar zigzagging across his face. He chased me, screaming, across a wide stretch of tall, green grass.

* * *

The following Friday, I sat with my head cradled in my hands, my elbows on the console. Nine days had passed since the local woman asked me to switch to a non-recording line. Eight days since I began answering each phone call with the hope it would be Jaku saying he needed a friend, and pleading for me to switch to the phone in the adjoining office.

"Sure," I planned to say as I pulled out the recording device and silently connected it to the phone. "Anything for a friend."

My disappointment at his not calling was tempered with the news from Carey that a recording device used without the prior approval of a judge could not be used as evidence in a court of law. "But the police can do a voice scan and determine beyond a shadow of a doubt if the voice belongs to Jaku," Carey said, perhaps in an attempt to soothe the disappointed detective in me. I resolved to keep trying for a recording anyway, because plotting gave me a way to fight the hopeless feeling of helplessness at my inability to help tip the scales against Jaku. This feeling hung like a black shroud over my heart.

In the evening, I sat with Tony, Tim, and Sam at one of the green vinyl-topped dining tables in the community room. "Any news about Jaku?" Tim asked.

"The last thing I heard was Greg and Morry ran into him at Bellows Beach," I said. "Three weeks ago." I wasn't about to mention the mysterious phone calls.

"Wish I knew what Jaku's up to now," Sam said, "and what the two of them were arguing about. The argument must have been going on for days before Jaku shot Vic."

"What makes you think so?" I leaned forward in anticipation of learning something, anything, to make the pieces of the puzzle fit together more snugly.

"Because Vic was on edge. He got into two arguments during the last couple of days before he was killed. Vic, the guy who made it a point never to let 'petty bullshit' get to him." Sam handed his dinner plate to a kitchen worker busing dishes. "Vic yelled at Keith in front of everybody for leaving Ramp 7 dirty. That wasn't like Vic. His way was to take a guy aside and talk to him one on one. Vic got into it with Peewee, too. Peewee was running one of his numbers, giving the firemen orders, you know how he does. Vic always ignored Peewee, pretended he wasn't there. But this time Vic told Peewee to shut up. Needless to say, Peewee shut up."

I thought about the morning before Vic was killed, when he'd stuck his large hands in my face and told me to "Look at the size of these hands." I imagine he was trying to tell me he was big enough and strong enough to protect me. And he was, from everything but a killer's bullets.

"The mystery is, what were they arguing about?" Sam forked out a chunk of cherry pie. "Vic said something to me the day before he was killed that really makes me wonder now." He stuffed a large bite into his mouth.

I squelched the "What? What?" trying to slip out of my mouth.

Finally, Sam continued, "He said Jaku would be back at work Friday even if he had to drag him there. I figured Vic was looking out for Jaku because the punk was going to be fired if he didn't come back to work then. When Jaku called in sick the Wednesday before, he spoke to the chief, who came down on him hard because he'd been taking so much sick leave. The chief ordered him to either show up Friday with a doctor's excuse or be fired. Jaku promised he'd be at work Friday. But maybe, considering Vic's remark, Jaku was planning to call in sick again."

"Interesting," Tony said. "I wonder what Jaku was planning to do on Friday if he wasn't coming to work."

I didn't say a word.

"Something Emilio told me made me think Jaku was going to come to work Friday morning to murder some of the supervisors," Tony continued. "Maybe some of us, too."

"What?" I asked.

"Jaku told Emilio on Monday he was going to call in sick on Wednesday and then come to work on Friday and 'blow some shirts and firemen fuckers away.' Excuse me, Liz." Tony frowned. "Since he did call in sick on Wednesday and was packing a loaded .357 Magnum on Friday morning, I figure that's what Jaku had planned. And Vic tried to stop him."

"Vic's neighbors heard Vic arguing loudly over the phone the night before he was killed," I said. "Unfortunately, nobody heard what he was saying."

Sam asked, "Does anybody know if Vic was scheduled to work on Friday?"

"He was," I said, "which makes me think Vic knew about the foul deed Jaku intended to do, and didn't want to go to work and leave Jaku free to do it. But if Jaku planned to shoot a bunch of people, it seems like the easiest way to do it would have been to show up at roll call when both shifts and the bosses were gathered together."

"Sounds to me like Jaku was lying. Again," Tim said. "On the one hand, he tells Emilio he's going to blow some of us away on Friday. But maybe he was just blowing off steam 'cause he always said he'd never commit a felony on a military base. 'No way is bruddah Jaku gonna do time in one federal pen,' he'd tell me."

"Say, Liz," Sam squinted at me, "You went out with Vic. And you and Jaku had some hassles, yeah? You sure there's not something you're keeping from us?"

"I only went out with Vic once, on a double date with Tony here." *Why should I tell him or Tim anything? They wouldn't tell the truth for Vic. There sits Tim, who witnessed Jaku pointing a loaded gun at Mad Max's head, not once but several times, and refused to tell the police. And Sam, who saw Jaku pointing a loaded gun at Vic under the table, and was too cowardly to tell Vic about it.* I added, "And I hadn't seen Jaku for six weeks before the murder."

"The chief hadn't seen Jaku for six weeks either, but Jaku may have been planning to blow him away. Some of us, too." Tony sighed. "Wish I knew the answers."

The only hint I was willing to give them was, "Whatever Jaku had planned was probably something horrible. And Vic was trying to stop him."

Sam nodded. "That would be just like Vic, always looking out for folks."

Tim scraped his chair away from the table. "Excuse me, gang. I'm gonna scoop out some more ice cream." He disappeared inside the kitchen.

I glanced at Tony, who was staring through the glass windows lining the community room's west wall, and followed his gaze. A golden and purple sunset lit up the sky above rows of airplanes parked on the west ramp. "Spectacular, isn't it?" he asked, a faraway look in his eyes.

I thought about the countless times Vic had given me a break from the alarm room so I could step outside and admire a particularly breathtaking sunset. The low-down blues grabbed me. "Sure is," I managed to say.

Tony must have heard something in my voice because he asked, "What woeful and woebegone thoughts are going through the head of my favorite dispatcher?"

I smiled at the words he'd borrowed from Vic. "I'm missing Vic." I blinked hard. "And thinking about how little we know about each other. We work together but lead such separate lives, rarely sharing what's inside our hearts and minds."

"Very philosophical." The faraway look returned to Tony's eyes. "And true."

Chapter 9

Tuesday, April 23, through Wednesday, May 15

Bright forks of lightning sizzled across the sky, followed quickly by booming claps of thunder. Rain blowing sideways spattered hard against the alarm room windows. A witch's night, wild and electric.

Judy, the midnight shift operator, clocked in at half past midnight because, she said, a power outage knocked out her alarm clock. I cursed my fate, to drive home late in a decrepit old Chevy with bald tires, loaned to me by a friend while my car was in the shop. At least the overtime would help me pay an unanticipated three hundred-plus repair bill to replace my VW's cracked exhaust manifold.

Dark clouds extinguished the light from stars and moon as the rusty Chevy skidded along an unlit stretch of highway between Whaler Air Force Base and Waipio Town. The AM/FM radio emitted only crackling, static sounds, so I turned it off. "Everything's gonna be fine," I whispered, and breathed deeply, and chanted "Om" again and again.

I relaxed a little, but only until a flash of lightning lit up a dark VW van parked on the right side of the road. In that incandescent moment, the sight of a rag knotted over the license plate seared itself into my brain.

Oh my god. I shook at the certainty this was the brown VW van Jaku had said belonged to his pals, the toughs who maimed anyone who crossed Jaku. The van, now parked on the roadside on my way home. The van told me Jaku thought I would take the stand on Vic's behalf and had therefore sent someone after me. My worst fear had come to pass.

How did they know I would travel this road? Had someone told Jaku where I'd moved? Were they on the lookout for my VW bug so they could chase me down, beat me up, kill me?

Fear shook me like a rag doll in a dog's teeth. My fluttering foot pumped the gas, making the old Chevy jump.

Strange how, as my heart raced faster, time seemed to slow down. I thought about Jet insisting, "Fear is just fear." But he'd also said my fear that Jaku would get even with me if I confronted him was reasonable. However, this fear was still a fear, and fear, I believed, was the antithesis of faith. Maybe Jet had been right after all.

Right or wrong, I was full to the gills and drowning in fear. Something inside me snapped open, and fear drained out, and anger rushed in to fill the gap. "Screw Jaku!" I yelled. "Screw his thugs! These assholes aren't going to defeat me without a fight." Somehow I managed to steady my foot on the pedal, and drive to the Wahiawa exit.

The nearest pay phone was a dark booth beside a greasy-spoon diner. I plunked a quarter in the slot and dialed 911. The calm voice of the woman police dispatcher was a sedative for my racing heart as I stammered about the brown van. When I asked her to dispatch an officer to check things out, she said in the same unruffled tone, "Did you see anyone inside the van, ma'am?"

I told her no, it was too dark, but I was involved in a murder case and the van's license plates were covered and didn't that seem strange? I mentioned Jaku's criminal friends and the strange phone calls I'd been getting since he made bail. When she asked if I'd told the investigating Homicide detective about this, I said, "Yes, and Detective Yamasato told me to call the police immediately if Jaku bothered me."

She agreed to send a patrol car and notify Jet in the morning if the police found anything.

I drove home by way of old, pothole-riddled Kamehameha Highway. My grip on the wheel relaxed as I thought, *how blessed I am not to be driving my VW bug.* I decided I owed Judy big time for making me so late the tough guys probably thought I'd taken a different road home. Which I resolved to do from here on out, taking the back roads, or staying at Carey's house on base.

My sleep was broken, and I woke up tired at six o'clock. Sipping coffee, I watched red-crested Cardinals and sassy Mynah birds hopping across the green lawn outside my condo. Built like a fortress, with locks on the sliding glass doors, protected with the loud bells of a security alarm, my concrete home was a haven only as long as Jaku didn't find out where I lived.

When I figured Jet would have made it to work, I dialed Homicide. "Yamasato," Jet answered in his no-nonsense cop voice that never failed to shake the cobwebs out of my thought processes and make me wonder what I'd done wrong. I asked him about the van and wished my heart would slow down.

"The police didn't find anything, Liz." His voice was uncharacteristically gentle.

I tried to speak but couldn't. Defenseless, I waited for him to speak.

"The van was already gone." His voice still kind.

I could have kissed him for acknowledging the van was really there. I hoped he also believed it wasn't just some random van made sinister by a hysterical woman's imagination. "I was driving a different car so Jaku's friends didn't recognize it," I ventured. "They probably got tired of waiting. It was past 12:40 a.m. when I drove by."

"You can't be sure those were Jaku's friends."

His words shattered my fragile hope. I restrained myself from saying, "Yes, I can. Yes, I'm sure." But he was right. I had no proof. And proof was obviously required by this detective who seemed to be a "just the facts, ma'am" kind of cop.

But was he? After I hung up the phone, I pondered this question. The rumor mill had him a devout Christian. I imagined the rumors were right because, when he'd asked me, "Would you tell the truth for Vic if he was your brother?" and seen me flinch, he'd said, "Oh, so you have a conscience." And when he took my statement he'd asked, "Does your conscience feel better now?" I wanted to find a way to tell him about Vic's spirit contacting me, and about my dream, but how?

I fell asleep rolling the question around in my mind. By the following morning, I had decided Jet just had to be a religious man and, because he was, I could confide in him. I figured the only option open to me was to write him another letter. Grabbing a writing tablet, I plopped down at the dining table. The words flowed quickly from my pen:

April 24

Detective Yamasato,

> *There are things I can't tell you as a detective. Things I can only tell you as one Christian to another so that you, at least, will understand. I know you told me not to write you any more letters, but this is part of my whole truth.*
>
> *The morning Vic Lazzarini was killed, I went home and prayed to God to send me a dream that would tell me what Vic and Jaku were arguing about. Last month, while I was looking through my dreams (I write them down), I found a dream I'd dreamed last year, on August 13, the very night my ex-boyfriend Billy moved to Maui, six months before Vic was killed. It was no ordinary dream. It was a vision of things to come!*

I relayed the dream story. How Jaku forced his way into bed with me and joked after he raped me. How a muscular man's arm came through the window, his hand lovingly touching my shoulder, letting me know he understood I hadn't invited Jaku in. I wrote:

> *That arm belonged to Vic Lazzarini! He died protecting me! He protects me still, in death as in life. I have felt his presence. His spirit still lingers on the earth.*
>
> *I know you're a religious man. You spoke with the voice of my conscience during those first weeks following Vic's death, when I struggled between fear and conscience. You helped me by hurting my conscience, so I told you what I knew about Jaku and Vic.*

Jaku has a friend in the station, a local boy. I told him lies—I'm living on base with friends now, and my ex-boyfriend is coming back—because I don't want him to know I'm living alone in my apartment. And I don't want Jaku sending someone to follow me home again. Jaku would have no qualms about killing me if he thought it meant he wouldn't have to go to prison—believe it! Jaku doesn't take responsibility for his actions. In addition to the crimes I've told you about, the firemen tell me he's committed lots of others. But it doesn't do any good for me to tell you about those, does it? Because they're only hearsay evidence.

Every time Jaku runs into a former coworker from the fire department, he tells them the argument was about me. I hope he tries to call me again at the station. If he does I'll be waiting for him with my recording device.

*Signed,
Lizbeth Hartz*

On the following day, during a quiet time in the alarm room, an impression of someone thinking about me with strong intention came over me. I closed my eyes and a picture of Jet entered my mind. His eyes were closed, a devout expression on his face, his mouth moving in prayer as he held my head gently between his hands.

That night, I dreamed I was in an interview room with Jet at the police station. Randy was there and said to Jet, "She's finally here."

"Yes." Jet smiled and cradled my hand in his.

Randy left and Jet played tapes he'd recorded of people's statements. "Listen to this one," he said. I heard a woman's voice telling a long, bizarre story. Later, when I wrote the dream down, I wondered if the woman was me.

Suddenly I heard what sounded like a scuffle outside of the room. Someone yelled, "Give me your money!" and what sounded like shots were fired. "Are those shots?" I screamed, frightened. "Is there a crime going on?" Jet shook his head and said, "Oh no, not in the station, Liz. That's cable TV."

The dream startled me out of sleep. I reached for the journal on my nightstand, scribbled in my dream notebook, and then lay back down. Sleep stubbornly refused to return so I rose from the bed, grabbed my journal from the bookshelf, plopped down into a dining room chair, and wrote whatever came to mind. It was a routine I'd followed on other sleepless nights, and often resulted in my being able to go back to sleep.

I wrote about how reassuring Jet's hand felt in my dream and how, only two and a half months earlier, Vic cradled my face with his hands and sent chills up my spine, on the day before my heart shattered like a china cup on a concrete floor.

My tears formed tiny puddles on the wooden table's dusty surface. My vision blurred until I couldn't see to write. "I keep going on these crying jags," I sobbed. "I haven't been myself since you died, Vic. I miss you. I feel so lonely." Too tired to fight, I surrendered to the waves of pain crashing through me, and felt wrung out but better when they receded. The last thing I remember before falling asleep was Carole King singing on the radio, "It's going to take some time this time."

* * *

Four days later, on Monday morning, I was playing a Seals and Croft record album I'd inherited from Vic when the phone rang.

A woman with a cheerful voice introduced herself as Susan Brown from the Victim and Witness Kokua Center. Since I was a potential witness, she wanted to meet with me before the trial. I gulped and agreed to bring any questions I had to our meeting.

The phone rang again. It was my dad, asking if I had any news about Jaku. What a coincidence, as I had just been thinking he was wrong about me not having to testify.

When I told him about my appointment with Susan, he asked if this meant I would have to testify. I said I didn't know, but promised to ask Susan how my statements could be used as evidence in court when they were all hearsay.

"As soon as you get back home, call me." My father easily switched to his take-charge mode. "If you have to testify, your mother and I will decide if you should move back home for a while, and I'll fly over there for the trial. And if you're in any danger from that nut case, I'm moving you lock, stock and barrel back to Nevada with us."

I could always count on my dad for support. I loved him for this, and for his caring and wanting to look out for me. Nevertheless, his words tied a knot in my stomach. *Why don't you ask me what I think of your plans for me?* I thought but didn't say. My father added, "You could always find another civil service job here in Nevada. Either that or I'll come to Hawai'i and shoot the son of a bitch."

I did not want my father to think I didn't appreciate his support, nor did I have the audaciousness to tell him I wanted to handle this on my own. "You're the best, Dad." I meant it, but my defensive shield was firmly in place. "Don't worry. The police will protect me." Instantly, I realized this was the wrong thing to say to my father.

Dad snorted and said, "Oh, horse feathers!"

Mom, who was listening in on the other line, said, "Your father wants to support you, Lizbeth." I told them I appreciated them being there for me. I meant it. Nevertheless, I wasn't going to let my dad usurp my choices.

I promised to call as soon as I returned home from my meeting with Susan. When I'd been a rebellious teen, mom had accused me of being incredibly stubborn at times. I certainly felt stubborn now, more determined than ever not to let anyone force me from my home. *Not even you, Dad. And certainly not that jerk Jaku.*

Three days later, on May Day, I faced Susan across her cluttered desk. "Will I have to testify?" I asked.

The perky blonde woman smiled and said, "Anyone who makes a statement to the police is a potential witness and is referred to us for counseling. We explain how the legal process works and inform you of your rights." She handed me pamphlets and diagrams with flow charts. I glanced at them as she continued, "This brochure explains what we at the Victim and Witness Kokua Center do. This is a felony case flow chart and this describes the relevant points for prospective witnesses. However, if you are subpoenaed, the prosecutor, Daniel Soon, will meet with you before you testify in court."

"But why would I be subpoenaed?" I squirmed in the uncomfortable plastic chair. "Aren't my statements hearsay and therefore inadmissible as evidence in court?"

"It all depends on what Mr. Cardoza's defense is," Susan said. "True, your statements are hearsay, but they're first-hand hearsay. They're what Christian Cardoza told you. If Mr. Cardoza's defense is he never committed any crimes besides this one, then you might be called to testify in order to discredit him. And the judge will decide whether or not your testimony will be admissible as evidence."

At last I understood why Jet had pushed me so hard to make a statement. "Can you tell me if anyone else besides, possibly, me will be subpoenaed from the fire station?"

"The three firemen who were at the preliminary hearing, Lino Badua, Mike Aguiar and Emilio Helikihi. Possibly Chief Green."

"Mike Aguiar's so scared, he's moving to Washington next week," I said. "Will he have to come back for the trial?"

Susan frowned and thought about it for a moment. "No, because he would just be corroborating the other firemen's testimonies."

"Quite a few guys at work are scared, so they won't tell the police anything. Jaku told them the same stories he told me and more, but nobody will make a statement."

Susan shook her head. "Too bad, because that's the best way to ensure Mr. Cardoza will be locked up and not out walking the streets again."

I didn't know if this was true or just the spiel the cops and now Susan gave victims and witnesses, but since full disclosure seemed like our best chance for seeing Jaku behind bars, I was all for it. "Yes," I said, "I want to see justice done."

"That's the spirit, Liz!"

I thanked her for the good information. Back at home, I phoned my parents, crossing my fingers like I used to do as a kid because it meant what I said didn't count. "Dad, I've got good news. You were right. I don't have to testify."

"Great!" Dad sounded relieved. "What did those people say? Why did they have you come down?"

I uncrossed my fingers. "They talk to all the people who've made statements because they're potential witnesses. But, in my case, since the statements I made are all hearsay evidence, they're not going to use me." Well, this might be true.

"I told you they couldn't use your testimony in court." Self-assurance filled my father's voice. "Then I won't have to fly over there."

Yes, this was exactly what I wanted. For the sake of my fragile sense of autonomy, I was determined to prevent my dad from calling the shots, even if I had to revert to my childhood ways of coping—doing what I wanted on the sly or lying to get my way.

Dad continued, "Is the trial still set for June 7?"

"Right now it is. But the defense can file for a continuance and try to have it postponed at any time. I was thinking, since I don't have to testify, maybe I won't show up at the trial." I figured saying "maybe" prevented my statement from being a total lie.

Dad's voice grew deeper. "Exactly what I was going to suggest."

As if I didn't know.

Dad added, "You don't want that nut case seeing you and thinking, 'She wants to see me go to prison.' You don't want him blaming you for anything."

No I didn't, but Jaku might be blaming me already and, anyway, nothing could have kept me away from the trial. Even so, I didn't want my parents to worry, which was why I'd kept the van incident from them and why I was lying to them now.

"We're so happy for the good news," Mom said. "Keep us posted on any new developments."

I promised I would, and I meant it. Well, sort of. As long as it wasn't the kind of news that would propel dad onto the next Honolulu-bound flight, determined to whisk me far away from Hawai'i's sparkling shores.

* * *

Four days later, when I arrived at work fifteen minutes before the 4 p.m. shift, Deputy Chief Bob told me an official-looking letter awaited me in the alarm room. The subpoena ordered me to testify regarding Victor Lazzarini's relationship with Christian Cardoza on 6-6-85, on behalf of the State of Hawai'i.

At the top of the letter was typed, "Please phone Deputy Prosecutor Daniel T.L. Soon at 523-4167 upon receipt of the subpoena."

My hand shook as I handed Bob the letter. "Looks like you're going to have your day in court," he said, placing a hand gently on my shoulder. "We'll all be behind you."

Oh my god. Cameras were in the courtrooms now. Should I rent a wig and wear a disguise so people wouldn't recognize me? When I voiced my fears to Bob, he laughed and said, "I doubt if they have cameras at every trial. I wouldn't worry about it."

I told him I didn't want Jaku's punk friends to know what I looked like, even if there were no cameras and his friends came solely to watch the trial. "And if I'm on TV, without a disguise I would never feel safe anywhere in Hawai'i again."

"Well, I suppose you should do what makes you feel comfortable." Bob tried to suppress a smile. "Just try not to look so bizarre everyone starts laughing when you walk into the courtroom."

Four days later, Bob closed the alarm room door behind us and asked, "What's the latest on the phone calls?"

"Nobody asked me to talk on a non-recording line again." Pointing at the recording device peeking out of my bag, I added, "I'm going to quit lugging that heavy thing to work. Maybe Greg has told Jaku I'm living on base now and he's given up on following me home. If so, why does someone still call and hang up when I answer?"

Bob sank into the back chair. "You think he's finding out if you're on duty?"

I nodded. "With Jaku's connections, it would be child's play for him to get on base. All he'd have to do is convince a friend with a base sticker to let him duck down in the back seat until the guard waves them through."

Bob rubbed his chin. "I suppose. But his lawyer undoubtedly told him to stay clear of the base, and he'd be in a world of trouble if he got caught."

"True," I admitted. "And rumor has it Jaku swore he'd never commit a crime on a military base. But I wouldn't put it past him to have his pals ambush me on base. Every night, when I leave here at midnight, walk through the unlit end of the garage, and push the door to the parking lot open, my can of mace is poised to squirt any attacking dog or human."

"Just wake me up, Liz," Bob offered. "I'll walk you to your car, don't mind at all. I'm used to waking up in the night anyway."

I thanked him but said I'd never hear the end of it from the rescue guys sharing his bunkroom if I woke them up at midnight just so he would walk me to my car, which was prominently lit by the bright lights in the parking lot. "But if anything unusual or spooky happens, I'll take you up on your offer."

A radio alarm in the barracks cut our conversation short. Bob ran out the door, saying we could continue our talk later. But things got busy and, after working a couple of emergencies, we both forgot. I didn't remember until around 10:30 p.m., after he'd fallen asleep in his bunkroom.

At midnight, as usual, I pointed my can of mace at sinister shadows as I walked to my car. I wished the trial was over yesterday, and Jaku locked behind bars for the rest of his life, but a month of angst and uncertainty awaited me before he had to face a judge. And then what? If he got convicted—please God—would closure follow? I wanted my life back. My patience had worn rice-paper thin.

* * *

Three days later, I stood in the deserted community room, pouring myself a cup of coffee, when Tony quietly walked up behind me and said, "Hi, Liz." I jumped and spilled coffee on the stained red carpet.

"A wee bit jittery, are we? Sorry. I didn't mean to startle you."

I laughed nervously.

Grabbing some paper towels, he helped me sop up the spill. "Did Irene mention you have an important message in the alarm room?"

I told him she'd been dispatching when I arrived. "What's it about?"

"Let's find out," Tony said.

In the alarm room, Irene pointed at a note and continued talking on the red fire phone. I read aloud: "In regard to subpoena for June 9, trial has to be canceled. New subpoena will be issued for trial date of July 11, 1985. If any conflict arises due to new date, contact Deputy Prosecutor Daniel Soon at 523-4167."

I wondered if my face looked as crestfallen as Tony's at the prospect of having to wait an extra month. "Why do you suppose they put it off?" I asked.

He shrugged. "Who knows? Maybe the courts are backlogged. Or maybe Jaku's lawyer needs more time."

I frowned. "Seems like the powers that be ought to tell us what's going on."

"Never happen," Tony said. "Our state of mind is the least of their worries."

"I just hope they don't postpone it again. My heart can't take it."

* * *

On Tuesday, May 14, I sat slumped on a patio chair in my PJs. I watched sassy Mynah birds hop across the emerald-green grass, and felt as lonesome as a new widow. All I could think of was Vic in his grave, my dreams buried with him. Jaku's flip-flops still flapped down streets Vic's shoes would never touch again. I would never walk briskly at Vic's side, trying to keep up with his longer stride. My chance for happiness had been killed by Jaku's rage, lust, and jealousy.

I sobbed, grateful the adjacent patios were vacant so no one could witness my grief. Would I die lonely, always dreaming of what might have been?

Come on, Liz, I coaxed myself. *Climb out of the hole you've fallen into.*

An idea flashed in my mind, and spurred me to don jeans and a T-shirt. I was heading out the door when the phone rang. Carey's cheerful voice inviting me to the beach with her and Peggy lifted my spirits. I would have welcomed their company, but I didn't want to subject my white body to the burning rays of Hawai'i's noon day sun. So I told her I was on my way to a costume store.

"What for? Halloween's nearly half a year away," Carey said.

When I explained I wanted to rent a wig to wear in court for when I testified against Jaku, she repeated, "What for?"

"Because they have cameras in the courtroom now." I felt foolish explaining. "I'm worried Jaku's syndicate friends will watch the trial, and see what I look like. I'd just feel safer wearing a disguise."

"Do you really think Jaku's friends would come after you?"

"If my testimony helps put him away, yes."

"Do you think he's a big-time underworld criminal?"

"No," I admitted. "But even if his pals are just petty criminals, they did beat up an airman's mom and brother. They'd hurt me, too, if they figured I was responsible for Jaku going to prison. The wig's just insurance . . . why are you laughing?"

"Sorry. It's just that you in a wig . . ." She laughed harder.

I laughed, too. "I just hope nobody in the courtroom cracks up."

"I'd better not go then," she teased. "But, like Jet told you, it doesn't hurt to take precautions. Sorry you can't come to the beach."

I agree to pick up some nose putty for her to rub on Peggy's little nose when she made her up as a pint-sized witch on Halloween.

The small, hole-in-the-wall costume shop displayed hundreds of wigs on white Styrofoam shapes, sitting like decapitated heads on wide wooden shelves. I tried on dozens before deciding on a long, straight-haired, mousy brown wig because the drab color wouldn't stand out. Another plus was it looked way different than my short, blonde, curly hair.

After reserving the wig for the week of the trial, and buying a small can of nose putty, I drove home. Was I going to extremes? I could always cancel the wig. And if I wore it at the trial, at least I would give my coworkers a laugh.

When I arrived at work on the following midnight shift, a second subpoena awaited me, this one for the week of August 9. "Another month's delay," I moaned. A typed note on the subpoena said to phone Deputy Prosecutor Daniel Soon's office to confirm receipt.

The next morning, I phoned his office. When he answered, I asked if I should make an appointment to see him.

"An appointment won't be necessary, Miss Hartz." His voice sounded cultured and kind. "I have decided not to use you as a character witness."

"Really?" I said. "But I just received a subpoena with an August date for the trial."

"The subpoena makes it possible for us to call upon you if we need you," he explained. "I am not planning to use you, however."

The fatigue I felt from fighting my body's desire for sleep over the past eight hours dissolved at this welcome news. I asked, "Is it possible to inform Jaku's . . . I mean, Mr. Cardoza's . . . lawyer that I will not be testifying against his client?"

"Miss Hartz, we are required to provide the defense attorney with a complete list of witnesses and have already done so. Your name was not included."

"Would you mind telling me why you decided not to use me?" Could it be because of the van incident? Was my well-being even a consideration?

A long pause ensued. Worry that the State might have a weaker case without my testimony tugged at my mind. I was prepared to argue, "I'm willing to testify. I've taken precautions, rented a wig, would even go into a witness protection program if it meant giving the State a stronger case against Jaku."

Mr. Soon said, "We think we can convict Mr. Cardoza based on the evidence at the crime scene."

Feeling as if a heavy weight had fallen off my shoulders, I hung up the phone. What do you know? I'd told Mom and Dad the truth after all. Well, at least about testifying. Not about watching the trial, though. I intended to sit through every moment of it.

Would Jaku's criminal compadres steer clear of the courtroom? I hoped I had nothing more to fear from those punks, and wondered if I needed a disguise just to witness Jaku's day in court. My last thought before falling asleep was I had plenty of time to think about it, and didn't need to cancel my wig reservation just yet.

Thursday, May 16 - Monday, September 9

During the next sixteen weeks, memories of Jaku scraped like sandpaper across my mind. Occasionally, a fireman would run into him at a beach or a bar. Jaku would shake the startled man's hand and say something like, "Hey, good to see you, brah. Sad business about Vic, yeah? Was self-defense, the haole came at me with a gun."

For a few days after an encounter with Jaku, the bringer of news would bask in the spotlight of celebrity-hood. We curious bystanders would cluster around as the storyteller relayed Jaku's every word and offered his opinion about whether Jaku seemed angry, sad, satisfied, or set on revenge.

Bob, Tony, the chief, most of the firemen, and I were disappointed when the trial was delayed yet another month, until finally it was scheduled for the week of September 10. The silver lining was being able to take a vacation in August, when I flew to Nevada to join my parents for a couple of stress-free weeks. Well, nearly stress free. I had to keep quiet about the van and the phone calls as well as the reassuring presence of Vic's spirit. I didn't want to worry my mom and dad, nor did I want them to think I'd taken up permanent residence in La La Land.

My father parked their trailer in a camp park deep in a thick pine forests. On chilly nights, we crouched around a fire, our bodies toasty warm in flannel shirts, thick socks, thermal underwear, and jeans. Gentle crackling sounds from burning wood, sizzling coal, clicks and calls from night birds keeping watch from overhanging trees, lulled and charmed us. The wind turned into an icy paintbrush that drew pink circles on our cheeks, noses, and ears. We roasted hot dogs, scraped blackened marshmallows off twigs and onto graham crackers, and declared these tastier than the finest pastries. The stars exploded overhead, a million twinkling thumbtacks piercing the ebony sky. We talked and joked about days gone by.

One frosty night, as we huddled around the campfire, my father revealed a spiritual side of himself I'd never seen before. This retired general turned jeweler had designed and cast a delicate cross of gold, each prong a tiny heart, with a diamond chip in the center.

"Some say a cross will protect you," he said, presenting me with a little black velvet case holding the glittering heart.

Deeply touched, I oohed and aahed and hugged him. He smiled and watched me hook the golden chain around my neck.

"Wear it at least as long as that nutcase you worked with is free," he said. This from a man who had refused to go to church on Sunday with Mom and us kids, and got a kick out of arguing with Jehovah's Witnesses, insisting Jesus was just a Jewish carpenter.

When I returned to work after two weeks away, the firemen seemed happy to have me back "in your cage where you belong," probably because they were relieved to have a respite from pulling my shifts. Most firemen disliked desk jobs, believing their rightful places were in the heat of action. I think they also disliked multi-tasking. Handling radios, phones, and equipment simultaneously when they transmitted, rang, and beeped in the alarm room could be nerve wracking.

During a rainy night in early September, less than a week before the trial, Tony and I speculated about whether Jaku's determination to beat the murder rap was making him anxious and therefore dangerous. The firemen had no news for me. Jaku, it seemed, had steered clear of them; at least the ones who would have talked to me about him. Greg, the young airman who was reputed to hang out with Jaku still, didn't volunteer any information. I dared not ask Greg anything lest it tip him off that his continued dialogue with Jaku was no secret.

September came squalling into existence one gloomy Saturday morning, on the heels of tropical storm Lani. She flooded the dry, leeward side of Oahu, and flung 30-foot waves against telephone poles lining the coast of Nanakuli and Waianae to the west. At Whaler, Lani sent on-call repairmen scrambling for sandbags to barricade doorways of low-lying houses against water running across yards and roads.

The very elements, they said, were agitated about the upcoming trial, and the gale-force winds blowing roofs off houses and uprooting trees were dispatched by the Devil.

At the station, things were smoking. Firemen rode their trucks through torrents of rain, checking out blown transformers and downed or sparking electrical power lines. Some of the guys thought the hurricane was an evil omen.

Fortunately, I possessed a talisman to combat evil. When fear and grief wrapped their tendrils around me, I remembered to rub chrism oil on my forehead, pray for the Lord's protection, and repeat the priest's words: "I believe in the Devil. But God is stronger." Then I visualized the Tree of Life, its roots extending deep into the earth's rich brown loam, its branches spreading wide and green into the sky. When I saw this tree clearly, I was able to relax enough to try and meditate. But, even then, my internal chatter usually prevented me from focusing.

On one occasion, however, when I somehow managed to let go and sink below my monkey-mind's incessant dialogue, my meditation transported me from agitation to peace. It was then I felt Vic's energy embrace me so ecstatically that my fear and sorrow dissolved like smoke in the trade winds.

* * *

On Sunday, September 8, I made it into the community room for dinner two minutes before the line closed. My pal Lino stood in line behind me, and lowered his muscular body into a chair beside me. Even before he'd voluntarily told Chief Green about Jaku bringing a loaded gun to the station, I had admired Lino for his devotion to Vic after Vic saved him from the rolling wheel of a C-5 aircraft. He had offered Vic, "Whatever you want, brah. My house, my car, anything but my wife, it's yours."

I was eager for conversation. Lino was, after all, half of the fireman twosome who would testify against Jaku, perhaps as soon as Monday. I gave him barely enough time to unload his dinner plate from his tray before asking, "So. How do you feel about having to testify?"

He frowned. "Not too good. When there were three of us guys, the prosecutor only needed two. Mike was supposed to be one, not me. Him and Emilio. But Mike ran off to the mainland. Like a dog, his tail between his legs. So now I've got to go in his place."

"You're not worried, though, right?" I could not imagine stalwart Lino being intimidated by the likes of Jaku.

He shook his head. "Nah. Long time ago, me and Jaku used to hang out, do stuff together. But then we had a beef. I told him, 'I know you, Jaku. Know how you operate, eh? Stay away from me, brah. I ain't your friend no more.'"

"You've got a lot of guts." Would things have been different if I had confronted Jaku as well? If I'd told him, "Jaku, you offend me. Get out and stay out of the alarm room," like Mad Max had told him—after which Jaku had taken to pointing a loaded gun at Max's head as he rode away on his bicycle. Yeah, things might have been different. I might have been dead.

"Jaku's not gonna do anything," Lino said. "If he sends some asshole after me, I can take care of myself. I'm not worried. But my wife is worried about the kids."

"I hope there's nothing to worry about, since all you have to do is testify you saw Jaku's loaded gun when he brought it to the station. Do you know the exact date the trial will start next week? I want to go."

"Nah. We won't know until the day before it starts."

"Does that mean it can't be tomorrow, since tomorrow will be Monday?"

Lino looked puzzled. "I'll leave word at the station as soon as I know. But I thought you were gonna testify, too."

"So did I. But the woman from the Witness Assistance Center told me, only if Jaku claimed killing Vic was the first crime he had ever committed would they need my testimony to show he was lying."

"So, Jaku must be planning to come up with some other story?" Lino asked.

I nodded. "I just hope he doesn't plead insanity because, if he did, he might get off. Anyway, I am so relieved. Mr. Soon said he's going to try for a conviction based on the evidence at the scene."

"Yep," Lino agreed. "That's what he's going for."

* * *

The next afternoon, when I walked into the alarm room shortly before four o'clock, Irene glanced up from the phone and pointed at a written note from Lino. I grabbed it and read: "Trial tomorrow, 8:30, Circuit Court, 777 Punchbowl, Courtroom #5, 4th floor."

Between phone calls, Irene filled me in on what was happening. I must have given her a blank stare because she asked, "Get that, Liz?" I had to admit I didn't.

She patiently repeated herself before heading off into the bumper-to-bumper traffic she would hit driving home. I anticipated getting stuck in heavy traffic the following morning as well, when I drove into Honolulu. God willing, the wheels of justice would carry Jaku away to prison. *Please God, be willing.*

I stopped by the costume shop after work and rented the long-haired, mousy brown wig.

CHAPTER 10

Trial Day 1, Tuesday, September 10

By six o'clock on the following breezy morning, I was inching my way through clogged city streets. Two hours later, I searched for a parking spot near circuit court. No luck. Three blocks further away, I found a spot.

I dumped quarters into the meter, my blue, tent-like muumuu ballooning around me, the edges of the floppy hat I'd worn over my wig flapping in the wind. Tucking a bag holding high-heeled shoes under my arm, I sprinted to the building. Three flights of stairs later, I arrived at the courtroom only to find it empty. When I hunted the court clerk down, she said the trial, now scheduled for 9 a.m., would take place in district court a few miles away.

I ran back to my car, inched through traffic to a parking garage near district court, and ran to the building. The escalator carried my tired body to the second floor, where four long hallways converged at right angles to an open space in the center. Since no one stood nearby, I crouched down and exchanged my flip flops for high heels. Uncertain of which way to go, I pulled my floppy hat down to hide my face.

A clock on the wall said two minutes until nine. I spotted Detective Randy Grabowski sitting on a bench opposite one of the courtrooms, shuffling through papers piled on his lap and spilling across the bench.

I headed his way. "Hello, Randy. You here to testify?"

He squinted at me until I flipped the brim of my hat up so he could see my face. Grinning, he nodded. "Me and Jet. How about you?"

"No." It surprised me he didn't know. "Mr. Soon said I don't have to."

"Just here to watch, then?"

I nodded. He snatched up some papers to clear a space for me. Not wanting to miss a moment of the proceedings, I remained standing, wobbling on my high heels. "Has it started yet?"

"No. There's been a delay." Dismay must have written itself across my face, because he hastened to explain, "The assigned judge is ill. They'll decide by 10 o'clock whether to assign another judge or cancel the trial for today."

Squelching a desire to scream, I thanked Randy for the update. At a pay phone on the first floor, I dialed Norma's number. No answer, just as there had been no answer the night before. Antsy and anxious, I replaced my high heels with flip flops and walked down the block to a coffee shop. The coffee tasted almost as bitter as I felt at the thought of seven months passing since Jaku killed Vic and now the trial might be postponed again. A few minutes before ten, I ran back, my caffeinated heart racing faster than my feet. Slipping inside a restroom, I stepped into my high heels.

Jaku and his parents stood beside one of the courtrooms. He didn't see me as he talked with his mother, an attractive woman with a thick black braid trailing down her back. Her husband, a stout man with a white shock of hair, stood beside her. For the first time, compassion for his parents washed over me. When they named their baby boy Christian, they undoubtedly hoped for a righteous son. How sad they must be.

Feeling faint, I sank down on a nearby bench, adjusting my hat so it hid more of my face. Jaku swiveled, his eyes scanning the hallway, stopping as they landed on me. For a moment, I quit breathing, but he didn't appear to recognize me. I looked past him, pretending not to see him, my heart pounding loudly in my ears. He turned to his mother and tapped her on the shoulder.

Taking advantage of his averted head, I turned my back to him and walked as quickly as my wobbly high heels would carry me to the rail separating the escalator from the hallway. Glancing downward, I saw Jet, briefcase in hand, taking the slow ride up, his gray eyes on me.

The sight of him pulled my mind away from the killer standing less than fifty yards away.

I pushed my hat backward so he could see my face, and gave him a small wave. He smiled, and I gratefully smiled back. Although I'd kicked and screamed at this brook-no-nonsense, perceptive detective's relentless insistence I tell the truth no matter the risk, I felt deeply indebted to him for cracking my dark shell of fear and confusion and pulling me, squalling, into the light.

I glanced back in the direction of the courtroom and sighed in relief. Jaku had disappeared. People were walking into the courtroom. I followed, pulling the heavy Koa-wood door open and hurrying inside. The icy air made goose bumps pop out on my arms, but my head was sweating under the hat and wig.

The same group of Jaku's family members and in-laws I'd seen at the preliminary hearing clustered together on the left side of the wood-paneled courtroom. Nobody who looked like a tough guy sat with them. Breathing more easily, I slid onto an empty bench behind Jaku's entourage. Even with no TV cameras in the courtroom, as the only person present who supported Vic, I felt safer wearing a disguise.

Three pretty women with creamy white skin whom I recognized as Jaku's sisters sat between his parents and the short man with angry eyes I'd seen at the preliminary hearing, the man Tony had said was Jaku's bad-ass cousin. He'd given me a "stink-eye" look then, but now he didn't appear to recognize me.

The fortuneteller thought Jaku had a good lawyer, and might get off. I fervently hoped this prediction was among the twenty percent she commonly got wrong.

In the front right quadrant of the courtroom, Jaku sat at a table next to the same short, stout Japanese lawyer who had represented him at the preliminary hearing.

Behind another desk, on the opposite side of the courtroom, sat Deputy Prosecutor Daniel Soon. He walked over to a man seated on a bench and spoke with him quietly. Soon stood nearly six feet tall and sported thick black eyelashes any women would envy. He looked so young. I hoped he was experienced enough to handle Jaku.

We all stood as the judge, an elderly man of Japanese heritage, walked into the courtroom. He stared at us through eyes magnified by thick glasses. I hoped he had read my statement, and been offended by Jaku calling Japanese people Buddha heads. No jury walked in. Why had Jaku waived his right to a jury trial? Had his attorney talked him into it? Did he think he'd have a better chance with a judge? I worried and wondered.

A detailed pencil drawing of Jaku's fourplex, showing a view of the building as seen from the street fronting his apartment, was tacked onto a portable poster board to the right of the judge's bench. The drawing showed the location of the two upstairs apartments, the two downstairs apartments, Jaku's on the left, and the open garage. The garage held parking spaces for four cars between the two downstairs apartments. At the back of the garage, a stairway led to the second story.

Two cars were parked in the garage when the shooting occurred—Jaku's black Toyota with its hood raised in the leftmost stall, and his upstairs neighbor's car in the third stall from the left. The second and fourth stalls were empty. An outline of Vic's body was sketched on the floor of the garage next to the Toyota. Vic's truck was parked sideways, blocking Jaku's car, at the entrance to the garage.

The first witness called to the stand, Ernesto Escalona, lived in the apartment directly above Jaku's and was the only neighbor home when Jaku shot Vic. Ernesto testified he'd heard two loud voices downstairs, arguing for three to eight minutes, but couldn't make out what the voices were saying until he heard the haole yell, real loud, "I hate you!"

"And then," Ernesto said, "I heard Jaku's, 'Fuck you, brah!' louder yet. And then I heard five or six gunshots, one right after the other."

"What did you do then?" Soon asked.

"I stood there shaking for a couple of seconds, wondering what for do now." A tremor crept into Ernesto's voice. "Then I walked down the stairs leading to the garage, slowly, 'cause I scared I going to get shot, too. Then I see the haole guy lying there on the garage floor, his head in a pool of blood."

"Did you see anything else?" Soon asked.

"Yeah. I saw the haole guy with his right hand on top his chest. He was gasping, breathing hard."

"Did he have a gun in his hand?"

Ernesto licked his lips and glanced nervously at Jaku before softly muttering, "No."

I smiled. Ernesto's testimony at the preliminary hearing had been he couldn't remember where Vic's right hand was because he was freaking out at the sight of so much blood. Rumor had it Ernesto was terrified of testifying against Jaku. Apparently, he was even more afraid of Jet. I could certainly understand why.

"And did you see Mr. Cardoza anywhere around?" Soon continued.

"No. So when I saw the haole guy lying there, I ran back upstairs, and call the ambulance."

"And what did they tell you?"

"They said, 'Call the police.' I was calling them when Jaku ran up the stairs and yelled at me, 'Hey, brah! Call the police. I shot this guy but he came at me with a gun.' I told him, 'Yeah, brah, that's what I'm doing, I'm calling the police.'"

"And then what did you do?"

"I stayed in my apartment until the detectives came and asked me what happened. So I told them, and they record me."

When the detectives had tape-recorded Ernesto in February, he told them Vic was not holding a gun. According to Chief Green, Jet threatened Ernesto with perjury if he didn't tell the truth during the trial. "Smart," the chief said, "to rush in and record folks while they're still shook up, before they have a chance to make up lies."

The cross-examination by Jaku's lawyer was long and drawn out. He kept repeating Ernesto's every word, and asking him if indeed this is what he intended to say. Ernesto kept saying yes, what he said was what he meant. The proceedings were so boring I almost nodded off, in spite of the goose bumps prickling my arms. After what seemed like hours, the cross-examination ended.

The next witness, a wiry painter named Ray Cambra, took the stand. "I was painting the second floor balcony of the apartment across the street," he said, "when I heard what sounded like a car backfiring four or five times. So I turned around. I spotted this guy crouching down, dragging something. I didn't have a good view because a red truck halfway blocked the driveway. So I couldn't see what the guy was dragging."

Ray continued, his voice smooth as silk, "I kept watching. After a few seconds, I saw the guy look all around, walk around the red truck to the street side, and climb into the truck on the driver's side. He was carrying what looked like a blue shirt, wadded up, in one hand. He wrapped something in the shirt, then got out of the truck with the shirt in his hand, and looked all around again." Ray's thin hands acted out the wrapping up, and his brown eyes mimicked nervously looking around. "Then he went back into the garage, and I couldn't see him anymore."

"And then what did you do, Mr. Cambra?" Soon asked.

The painter shrugged. "I went back to painting the balcony. A little while later, all these police cars arrived. I walked across the street and found out somebody had been killed. So I told the police what I'd seen."

I admired Ray's composure when Jaku's lawyer repeated the same questions over and over during the cross-examination. Several times the judge said, "The witness has already answered the question, Mr. Nozawa." At last, the judge called a recess for a late lunch at 1:30 p.m.

A phone call to Fire Chief Green confirmed what I suspected—several of the firemen tried to watch the proceedings but found an empty courtroom. "I appreciate your resourcefulness, Liz," he said, and promised to announce the trial had been switched to District Court. "Tomorrow, a lot of our guys will be there."

Oh, good. I would leave my wig home tomorrow. That way, the firemen wouldn't explode into laughter at the sight of me, and maybe tip off Jaku's group that the long-haired woman who sat behind them today had been a Vic-sympathizer in disguise.

I dialed Norma's number, but there was still no answer. I walked to a restaurant across the street and guzzled down another strong cup of coffee in hopes it would help me stay awake through Nozawa's dull cross-examinations.

When the trial resumed, Officer Grace Classon, the first police officer to arrive at the scene, took the stand. "Mr. Cardoza was going on and on, talking nonstop, when I arrived at the scene," Classon said.

"What did he say?" Soon asked.

"Mr. Cardoza claimed Mr. Lazzarini sped into his driveway in his truck, parked sideways so Mr. Cardoza could not drive out, and yelled at him, waving a gun." She paused.

"Go on, Officer Classon," Soon instructed.

"Mr. Cardoza said he then ran into his apartment, grabbed his own gun, stuck it in his trousers, and rushed back out. At this point, he said, Mr. Lazzarini came running at him from the opposite side of the garage, his gun pointed at Mr. Cardoza. So he, Mr. Cardoza, pulled out his gun, and shot Mr. Lazzarini in self-defense. The accused told me Mr. Lazzarini had called him on the phone earlier, saying he was coming over, but he, Mr. Cardoza, didn't expect anything like this. Mr. Cardoza also told me he tried to give Mr. Lazzarini CPR after he shot him, but it didn't do any good."

"Did you advise Mr. Cardoza of his rights?" Soon asked.

"Yes sir, as soon as I arrived on the scene. He said he didn't care, he was all shook up because this guy came at him with a gun, and he was scared, and this kind of thing didn't happen every day, and he wanted to talk about it."

"Where was Mr. Cardoza's gun when you arrived at the scene, Officer Classon?"

"Lying on the front bumper of Mr. Cardoza's Toyota."

"In what position was the hood of Mr. Cardoza's car?" asked the prosecutor.

"The hood was up."

Several police officers who had arrived at the scene after Officer Classon testified next, relating in detail what they had seen and done. In spite of my earlier coffee, I had to pinch myself to remain awake.

Nozawa tried to find instances of improper procedure on the part of the police. He failed.

After the police officers finished testifying, four police technicians involved in taking fingerprints and photographs testified and told in great detail how they did their jobs, what they looked for, and what the Homicide detectives had instructed them to do. When the judge adjourned for the day at 5 p.m., I wanted to run out of there.

However, the promise I'd made to Norma five months previously motivated me to wait downstairs for the first available pay phone. We had been reminiscing about Vic when she'd said, "I felt like he was my grandson. After my husband passed away last September, he helped me in so many ways, picking up my groceries, offering to take me places since I don't drive, stopping by to check on me. Now there's one thing I want to do for him."

When I asked her what the thing was, she replied, "See his murderer convicted." I'd promised to call her as soon as I found out the trial date and place, but here she was missing the trial. Without much hope, I plopped my last quarter into the slot. This time she answered. I told her what had happened in court and asked, "Will you come with me to the trial tomorrow? It starts at nine."

"Well, of course, dear!" Her exuberant voice lifted my spirits. "I would have come today if I'd known. I can't wait to see the jury convict that little worm."

"There's no jury, just a judge. Jaku must have waived his right to a jury trial. Don't you think it's strange? Seems like a judge would be tougher than a jury."

"Good! No jury means we've got a better chance of watching the creep get what he deserves," Norma said enthusiastically. "I'll meet you at the courtroom at 9 o'clock, dear. No need to pick me up. I enjoy my morning walk."

Trial Day 2, Wednesday, September 11

When I stepped off the escalator at District Court, the sight of half a dozen firemen, most accompanied by wives or girlfriends, welcomed me. The firefighters peppered me with questions about what happened the previous day. I repeated what Jaku's neighbor and the painter had said, imitating the latter's depiction of Jaku climbing in Vic's truck, his eyes darting around like pinballs.

Smiling at my pantomime, Morry asked no one in particular, "You think Jaku was on speed?"

"Or maybe cocaine," Jack speculated.

Tony said, "I wonder if the cops tested him for drugs."

"What do you suppose Jaku did with his stash?" Brian asked.

Pete said, "Jaku probably flushed it down the . . ." then stopped talking as Jaku's family rounded the corner, strode past us without a word, and entered the courtroom. Just as silently, our group followed.

Jaku's family and friends sat on the left side of the courtroom. We sat on the right. I spotted Norma's snowy hair a few rows in front of me. She sat ramrod-straight, alone until I slipped onto the bench next to her. Her blue eyes sparkling, she smiled and squeezed my hand. "Brr! It sure is cold in here," she said.

I swallowed hard, grateful for the friendship of this woman whose love for Vic and disdain for Jaku paralleled my own. "Darn! I should have warned you."

Tony and Annie squeezed past my knees and sat beside me. The rest of the fire folk sat clustered around us. "I'm glad Vic's friends are here," I told her. "I felt so alone yesterday."

Norma clucked sympathetically. "When you feel alone, ask the Lord to be with you, and He will make His presence known. He's here all the time, you know." She pointed her chin at Jaku, fidgeting in a chair at the front of the courtroom. "That little worm is the one who's really alone."

Firefighter Lino Badua testified first. He said he had seen Jaku brandish a .357 Magnum at the fire station the previous December.

"Was the gun loaded?" Soon asked.

"Yes, sir, it was."

"How do you know it was loaded?"

"Jaku opened up the chamber and showed me the bullets," Lino said.

Soon pointed to a gun, tagged and labeled as Exhibit A. "Is this the same weapon you saw at the fire station last December?" he asked.

"Yes, sir."

During cross-examination, Jaku's lawyer asked Lino, "Are you sure this is the same weapon you saw at the fire station in November?"

"December," Lino corrected him. "No, sir, I can't be sure. It looks like the same weapon though."

Emilio Kelikihi testified next. His testimony was identical to Lino's. Again, Nozawa asked, "Are you sure this is the same weapon Mr. Cardoza brought to the fire station?"

"No." Emilio glanced nervously at Jaku. "I'd have to know the serial number to be sure."

The next witness, Mr. Jefferson, a puffy-eyed ballistics expert, said, "Four bullets from Mr. Cardoza's gun lodged in the body. The remaining two shots were fired into the concrete floor next to the body. The impact of those two bullets caused fragments of concrete to shatter in an oblate spheroid pattern." He paused, giving us time, I imagined, to decipher his words before continuing. "The fragments lodged in the deceased's body in a pattern consistent with his right hand resting on his chest."

Jefferson stared at the audience. I whispered to Tony, "Oblate spheroid?"

"A flattened sphere," Tony said, "three dimensional, sort of like a blimp pattern."

Jefferson continued, "It would have been impossible for the cement fragments to lodge in the upper section of the right arm in the pattern they did, had the right arm been extended out from the body." He paused before adding, "Another discrepancy. When we lifted up the right arm of the deceased, we found concrete fragments on the back of his arm. We surmised the right arm had to be moved after the bullets were fired into the concrete in order for those fragments to be there. Your Honor, I have a series of slides to illustrate my points. I request your permission to show them now."

The bailiff wheeled in a white, chalkboard-sized screen and turned off the lights. The first slide, a close-up of the right side of Vic's body, showed fragments of concrete lodged in his right arm and torso.

At the sight of so many small, bloody wounds in Vic's arms and sides and a gaping wound in his chest, I wanted to cry and scream and jab my nails into Jaku's neck.

Norma whispered, "I don't want to see our Vic like that."

I whispered back, "Me neither."

Stomach acid spurted into my throat. *Oh, God, don't let me throw up.* I breathed deeply several times and averted my eyes from the screen while Jefferson clicked through the slides. He explained how he calculated the pattern of dispersal of the concrete fragments based on the angle of the bullets striking the concrete, and the location and concentration of fragments in Vic's body.

Dr. Ingram, the medical examiner for the State of Hawai'i, testified each of the four gunshot wounds was surrounded by stipple marks caused by powder burns.

"These indicate all four shots were fired from very close range," Ingram said. "Between twelve and eighteen inches from the body."

I quietly said to Norma, "Sounds like they were arguing face to face."

She answered, "It surely does. Jaku must have concealed his gun."

Ingram continued, "The first shot penetrated the deceased's chest and lodged in his spine, paralyzing him from the chest down, and causing his death." He described how Vic started to fall forward as the shots were fired into his body in rapid succession. "But the impact of the fourth shot to the top of his head caused his body to jerk and fall backward, so he came to rest on the floor of the garage on his back."

Again, color slide after color slide clicked across the makeshift screen, showing close-ups of the bullet wounds in Vic's body. Again, Norma and I looked away.

After Dr. Ingram stepped down, Detective Randy Grabowski took the stand. "The victim was found with a perfect grip on the weapon, index finger still on the trigger, fingers wrapped around the gun. Very unusual."

"Why unusual?" Soon asked.

"Most of the time, the gun falls out of the hand when a man falls from a standing position."

"Did you find anything else unusual?"

"Yes. There was blood on the palm of the right hand, but no injury to the fingers, as would normally be the case if a hand hit the concrete holding a gun. And the gun in the deceased's hand was a broken pellet gun that would not fire."

What!? Jaku planted a broken gun in Vic's hand!? My jaw dropped. I locked eyes with Norma. She frowned and shook her head.

During cross-examination, Jaku's lawyer asked Grabowski, "Did you search Mr. Lazzarini's apartment?"

"Detective Yamasato and I looked through his apartment."

"Did you find any marijuana there?"

"No, sir." Grabowski frowned. "We did not."

"Did you find any weapons?" Nozawa asked.

"Yes. A .38 caliber pistol was lying on the deceased's bed."

Randy stepped down. I whispered to Norma, "Neatly made bed, according to Tony. Vic must have considered taking his own gun. I'll bet Jaku was threatening to blow him away, but Vic couldn't believe he'd really do it. And . . ." I closed my mouth at the sight of Jet striding to the stand.

He was a study in black—thick, slicked-back hair, tailored suit and matching tie. His stern expression and the intensity of his gray eyes had me thinking, *Executioner or saint?* His integrity and competence made me admire him immensely.

"Right away I saw there was evidence of foul play," Jet said.

"What evidence?" Soon asked.

"Firm grip on the gun. Blood on the right hand but no injuries to the fingers. Four shots in the body and two in the pavement."

During cross-examination, Nozawa asked, "How many homicides have you investigated, Detective Yamasato?"

"Roughly 250 to 300." Jet's eyes scanned the audience, as if Nozawa's questions were too insignificant to command his attention.

"Do you think this qualifies you as an expert?" Nozawa raised his eyebrows, a skeptical expression on his face. "Have you gone to school to learn the proper way to conduct an investigation?"

"I'm a professional!" Jet said angrily.

"Answer the question, detective," the judge ordered. "Counsel has the right to establish credibility and the proper credentials."

Jeff rolled his eyes. "Yes, I've gone to several schools."

Bob had told me about Jet's reputation for speaking his mind to witnesses, judges and lawyers alike, and for not suffering fools gladly. As he faced Jaku's lawyer during the cross-examination, they seemed like two samurai with katanas gleaming sparks, slashing at each other. But one of them kept missing the mark.

"Do you think this qualifies you as an expert witness?" Nozawa asked.

Jet frowned. Soon hopped up from the chair. "Objection! Counsel has already asked the question. He is badgering the witness."

"Objection sustained. Mr. Nozawa, this court recognizes Detective Yamasato as an expert witness."

A smile played at the corners of Jet's mouth.

"Did you check the deceased's apartment for drugs?" A brittle edge crept into Nozawa's voice.

"Not specifically. My partner did most of the searching of the apartment."

"Did you find any drugs?" Nozawa asked.

"No."

When Jet stepped down, the judge declared the court recessed until 2 p.m. Tony escorted Norma and me across the street to a crowded restaurant.

"Is an oblate spheroid a three-dimensional elliptical pattern?" Norma asked. "And does this prove Vic's hand was on his chest when the shots were fired?

Tony nodded. "Smart, you. Yes to both."

"We're lucky the police are so sophisticated in their techniques," I said.

"And Jaku so dumb. Planting a broken gun in Vic's hand! But his stupidity shouldn't surprise anyone." Norma shook her head. "After all, he's nothing but a worm." She looked so serious we laughed.

The first person to testify after lunch was Detective Paul Lee, a portly man with dark circles under his eyes.

"Tell the court about your part in the investigation, Detective Lee," Soon said.

"To fingerprint Mr. Cardoza and inventory his personal belongings before he was transferred into the cell block," Lee said.

"Describe what transpired with Mr. Cardoza on February 14th of this year," Soon instructed.

"Officer Classon brought Mr. Cardoza to me for fingerprinting," Lee answered. "He was going on and on about how this big guy came at him with a gun. I advised him of his rights, and told him my only part in this case was to hold his personal possessions in custody and fingerprint him. He said, yeah, he knew his rights, but the guy he shot had syndicate connections, and he was afraid for his life, and wanted to talk about it."

"Did you tell Mr. Cardoza he had the right to remain silent?" Soon asked.

"Yes, sir, I did."

"Did you ask Mr. Cardoza what had transpired that morning?"

"No, sir, I did not. Mr. Cardoza volunteered this information. I interrupted Mr. Cardoza to advise him of his rights, and he said he already knew his rights."

As before, Nozawa's long and repetitive cross examination generated yawns in the audience. It seemed like hours before Lee finally stepped down.

Nozawa turned to the judge. "Your Honor, my client, Mr. Cardoza, would like to testify in his own behalf at this time. He has been advised he is not required to testify but has volunteered to do so nonetheless."

The judge raised his eyebrows. After a long pause, he nodded. "Very well, Mr. Nozawa. Mr. Cardoza, you may take the stand."

Jaku slowly stood up, shoved his chair away, took a deep breath, and squared his shoulders.

I whispered to Norma, "Do you suppose he's looking forward to standing in the limelight? Why else would he testify when he doesn't have to?"

Norma, who had worked as a paralegal, answered, "He must think he's got an ironclad case. Testifying in your own behalf is an all-or-nothing gamble."

Jaku bridged the distance between his seat and the stand with a couple of strides. His black eyes shimmied as he scanned the faces of the spectators and was sworn in.

His lawyer said, "In your own words, Mr. Cardoza, describe the events leading up to the shooting that occurred on February 14th of this year."

The white-knuckled clasp of Jaku's hands on top of his protruding stomach was clearly visible. In spite of the Arctic-cold room, sweat beaded on his forehead. He unclasped his hands. Pulling a white handkerchief from his jacket pocket, he wiped his forehead. "Well," he said, and paused, and repeated, "Well."

He swallowed hard, his Adam's apple bobbing, before continuing, "See, me and Lazzarini, we were having a disagreement. In January, me and him were fooling around, and I took some Polaroid shots of him. They were, well, I guess you could say they were obscene pictures. Right away, I showed them to Lazzarini, and he wanted them. But I told him, 'No way, brah.' So, a couple of times after that, he told me I'd better give him those pictures or else. I told him, 'Nah, no way. Or else what, brah?'"

Jaku shoved the handkerchief back in his pocket and rubbed his hands together. "So, a couple more times, he told me I better give him the pictures. I told him *no way* again. So, I was driving home on Wednesday, the night before the shooting, waiting at the red light at the corner of Prosper and Warren. All of a sudden, boom! Something hit my car from behind, real hard.

Ignoring the sweat sprouting on his forehead, Jaku said, "I looked behind me, all ready for scrap you know, and whoeee! I saw Lazzarini's red truck behind me. He was giving me the finger—" Jaku acted out the gesture with the middle finger of his right hand. Before the judge could call him down, he clasped his hands again and went on "—and yelled at me, 'Get your ass over to my place, brah!'

I was real shook up, you know, but I drove over to the guy's pad.

He beat me there, and when I walked to his front door, he was standing there smoking a joint. He yelled at me, 'You better give me the pictures, or I'm going to punch your face.'

"So I told him, 'Wait one minute, brah. Can we talk about this?' So I went inside, and the two of us rapped for a while. Before too long, Lazzarini calmed down. Well, then we got to drinking a couple of beers, and the guy wasn't pissed off no more.

After a while, he told me he liked my pellet gun, and asked me if he could trade something for it. I told him, "Brah, the gun's broke," but he said, "No sweat, I know somebody who can fix it." Well, that sounded okay to me, and I told him I liked this camera of his, and he said okay, he'd trade the camera for the gun. So I went downstairs, got my gun out of my car, and traded with him. A little while later, I went home."

Jaku paused, glancing around the courtroom, and swallowed hard. "The next morning, I was standing outside in the garage, pouring some water in my radiator, ready to drive to work, when, 'Boom!' Outta nowhere Lazzarini came screeching into my driveway, driving fast. He pulled up sideways, trapping me inside my garage so I couldn't get out. I yelled, 'Hey, brah, what you doing, man? I gotta go work, and the chief gonna be real pissed off at me if I'm late.'"

"But Lazzarini never like listen. He yelled, 'You fuckin' Portagee, I want those pictures!' Then he jumped out of his truck. He had a gun in his hand, and he pointed it at me. I'm telling you, I was all shook up 'cause I figured it's his .38 pistol, you know? I never knew it was the pellet gun. So I ran inside my apartment, grabbed my gun, stuck it inside my belt, and ran back into the garage. Lazzarini ran at me yelling, 'You punk! I want those pictures!' and raised the barrel of his gun at me."

With the back of his hand, Jaku wiped away the sweat dripping into his eyes. "I was all shook up, you know. It doesn't happen every day. When I saw that gun barrel aimed dead at my face, I made a quick draw, pulled my gun out, and fired it." Jaku arranged his fingers into a pretend gun, and acted out how he had pulled it from his waistband, quickly raised it to waist level, and fired.

He rubbed his hands together and continued, "When Lazzarini fell to the floor, I was all shook up, so I stood there, maybe for a minute, minute and a half, wondering what to do, and I wiped some blood off my hands. Then I walked over to Lazzarini's truck to check if he had more weapons. Then I wrapped up my firemen's shirt, thinking maybe I could make a compress bandage for the guy, but then I figured, 'No, maybe I better not touch the body.'"

"Then I thought maybe I better call an ambulance, so I climbed the stairs at the back of my garage, and told Ernesto to call the police and an ambulance. So then I put my shirt back on and waited for the police." He swallowed hard. "As soon as I saw a police car, I flagged the officer down. It was a lady, Officer Classon. I told her what happened, and she told me my rights. Then another police car came, and they took me to the police station."

Jaku paused, scanning the room. He coughed. "When I got to the police station, they took me to this Detective Lee, and he said, 'Hey, what happened over there?' So I told him, 'This guy came at me with a gun, and I shot him in self-defense.' Then he told me about my rights, and took fingerprints, and took the stuff in my pockets." Jaku took a deep breath. "That's about it."

Judge Fukuda's thick glasses magnified his brown eyes. "You may now cross-examine the witness, Mr. Soon," he said. The prosecutor stood up slowly. He strode across the floor, back and forth in front of the judge, crooking his left arm until the back of his left hand rested on the small of his back.

Abruptly, he stopped, brought both hands forward, palms upturned in a questioning gesture, and faced Jaku. "Why did you keep shooting at Mr. Lazzarini after you had already stopped him with the first bullet, Mr. Cardoza?"

Jaku shrugged. "He was still pointing the gun at me."

"Oh really?" Soon's eyes widened. "Before you put the fourth shot in his head, as he was falling, he was still pointing the gun at you?"

"Yeah. Like I told you." Jaku frowned as titters came from the right side of the courtroom. "He was down on his knees, but still pointing the gun up."

"Amazing," Soon said. "And what did you do after you shot him, for that minute or minute and a half, before you walked over to his truck?"

Jaku glared at Soon. "I just stood there and wiped the blood off my hand. Doesn't happen every day, you know." A tremor entered his voice. "I was all shook up. Even now, just thinking about it, you know."

Soon looked puzzled. "How did the blood get on your hand, Mr. Cardoza?"

"I . . . I . . . I . . ." Jaku stuttered, "I put my hand on his chest when he was lying on the floor, and tried to stop the blood. But then I thought, hey, maybe I shouldn't touch the body."

"So what did you do during that time, Mr. Cardoza?"

Not a whisper was heard in the courtroom. Soon paused for a full minute before saying, slowly and deliberately, accentuating every word, "Did you watch him die?"

Jaku opened his mouth, but no words came out. Silence echoed through the room. Finally, he said, "Well, I saw he was breathing hard, gasping. I couldn't think straight, didn't know what to do, so I ran over to his truck and looked inside for weapons."

Soon raised both hands in a questioning gesture, "Were you afraid, Mr. Cardoza, that Mr. Lazzarini might get up and come at you with more weapons?"

Jaku shrugged. "I was just curious, you know. So after I took a look inside the truck, I wrapped up my fireman's shirt, thinking I was going to make a compress bandage for the guy. But when I walked back over there he wasn't breathing."

"I see." Soon lowered his head, rubbed his chin, and strode back and forth in front of the witness stand before stopping and asking, "After you saw he wasn't breathing, you decided to go upstairs and ask your neighbor to call an ambulance and the police?"

"Yeah, like I told you before." Jaku squinted at Soon.

"I see. Now, Mr. Cardoza, you stated, when Officer Classon turned you over to Detective Lee at the police station for fingerprinting, he asked you what happened over there?"

Jaku nodded. "Yeah. So I started to tell him about it, and after a while he says, 'Wait a minute, I got to advise you of your rights.' Then he read me my rights."

Soon raised his eyebrows high. "You're saying, then, that Detective Lee did not advise you of your rights until after he had asked, 'What happened over there?' Is this correct, Mr. Cardoza?"

"Yeah. Like I told you before," Jaku said impatiently.

Soon turned his back to Jaku and faced the judge. "Oh, really, Your Honor! A police detective asking, 'What happened over there?' before advising an individual of his rights. Obviously, Mr. Cardoza is lying. As you know, Your Honor, when it can be shown that any part of an individual's testimony is false, the entire testimony can be discredited."

Soon took a deep breath before continuing, "Mr. Escalona testified he heard an argument for three to eight minutes, yet Mr. Cardoza says Mr. Lazzarini rushed at him with a gun, yelling racial insults, but said nothing about an argument. Mr. Cambra testified he saw Mr. Cardoza crouching down, dragging something. Furthermore—"

"Objection!" Jaku's lawyer shot to his feet.

"Yes, Mr. Nozawa?" the judge asked.

"Counsel has made no mention of the motive in this case. The fact is, the deceased came over to my client's apartment to confront him. He was the aggressor here, not my client."

"Your Honor," Soon countered. "As Mr. Nozawa should know, in 1972 the Legislature, in its wisdom, passed into law the decision that establishment of motive is irrelevant and immaterial in a murder case, based on the knowledge that what is significant is whether a murder did in fact occur. Which I will show, Your Honor."

"Objection overruled. Proceed, Mr. Soon," the judge instructed.

"Most of the credit for solving this case goes to the police department for their technical expertise under the direction of the Homicide Division." Soon punctuated his words with sweeping arm gestures. "The evidence clearly shows Mr. Lazzarini's right hand was moved. Mr. Escalona testified he saw the victim's right hand on his chest, no gun in his hand, when he walked down the stairs. The pattern of the fragments extracted from the body confirms Mr. Lazzarini's right arm lay across his chest when the fifth and sixth shots were fired into the pavement."

Soon spun around and looked directly at Jaku. "You went looking in Mr. Lazzarini's truck hoping to find his gun so you could plant it into his hand. But Mr. Lazzarini wasn't like you. He had no weapon because he had no intention to shoot anyone. So you had to run into your apartment to get your own broken pellet gun and place that in his hand instead."

Hunched over in the witness stand, Jaku dabbed at his forehead with his soggy handkerchief and glared.

Soon turned to the judge. "Imagine, Your Honor! Mr. Cardoza testified Mr. Lazzarini was still pointing the gun at him after the first shot. But the ballistics experts have testified the first shot lodged in the victim's spine and paralyzed him."

The prosecutor punctuated his words with sweeping arm gestures. "Obviously, Mr. Cardoza's entire testimony is fabrication. He might have been able to get away with this a hundred years ago, when his quick-draw story might have been believed, but not today." Soon pointed at Jaku. "Find him guilty, Your Honor, of murder in the first degree!"

"As it is now 5 o'clock, I will give my verdict tomorrow," Judge Fukuda said. "Court recessed until 10 a.m." The sound of his gavel was a fitting counterpoint to our silent stares upon the killer. Everyone stood as the judge exited the courtroom. Two big Samoans led Jaku away.

"Tomorrow?" I complained to Norma as we walked, shivering, into the hallway. "I wanted to hear the verdict today."

"Maybe the judge needs time to prepare his arguments," Norma said. "Isn't the prosecutor terrific?"

I agreed he was. We rode the escalator to the first floor and I offered Norma a ride. "Thank you, dear," she said. "Normally I'd walk, but looking at that ugly little worm all day has plum tuckered me out. I'll brew a pot of chamomile tea when we get home."

We sat at Norma's oak table and batted the day's events around as we sipped tea and nibbled her moist, homemade banana bread. A comfortable silence enveloped us. The last thing I expected was for tears to spill down my cheeks. Unable to stop their flow, I covered my face with my hands and sobbed. Norma moved her chair next to mine and wrapped an arm around me. "Don't cry," she said.

"All . . . all of a sudden, I . . . I . . . feel so sad," I stuttered. "Seeing Vic like that . . ."

Norma asked softly, "Has anybody else who you were close to died?"

"Just . . . my mom's mom," I sniffled.

"Only one grandmother? Well, that's a big difference between you and me. I miss Vic too, but life has to go on. Grief hurts, but it'll get better as time goes on. You'll see."

Her words comforted me. We hugged. Golden sunlight streaming through the living room's west window turned dusty rose. Sunset. Time to be on my way.

Norma pressed a foil-wrapped loaf of banana bread into my hand. "Keep your chin up, dear. I'll see you in court tomorrow."

The air chilled me on the drive home. The quiet rooms of my condo echoed with loneliness. Oh, if only Vic were alive and all of this a bad dream. I couldn't sleep, so I rolled off my futon and reached for my journal. Many words and tears later, I fell asleep around 2 a.m.

Still sleepy five hours later, I washed an oatmeal breakfast down with strong coffee. The caffeine made my heart race. God willing, it would keep me awake while I watched Jaku receive the life sentence for first degree murder.

Trial Day 3, Thursday, September 13

The courtroom held a dozen more Whaler firefighters than the day before. Again we sat on the right side of the courtroom, and Jaku's family sat on the left. Everyone stood when the judge walked in.

No sooner had we sat back down than Judge Fukuda said, "Please stand for the sentencing, Mr. Cardoza."

Jaku rose and faced the judge.

Fukuda said he was making his determination on Jaku's plea of self-defense based solely on the evidence. "I reviewed all of the technical evidence, the testimony of the witnesses, and your own testimony, Mr. Cardoza." He stared at Jaku through his thick glasses. "After a thorough review, I found innumerable discrepancies, not only between your testimony and the technical evidence, but also between your testimony and that of the other witnesses.

"I will recount some specific examples. Dr. Ingram, the medical examiner, stated all the bullets were fired from a distance of 12 to 18 inches from the body. Whereas you, Mr. Cardoza, testified Mr. Lazzarini came toward you from across the garage, raised his gun, and you fired on him from a distance. Mr. Escalona testified he heard an argument for three to eight minutes, whereas you testified Mr. Lazzarini rushed toward you and you shot him, but there was no argument. Mr. Escalona further testified, when he came down the stairs into the garage, he saw Mr. Lazzarini's right hand on his chest, no weapon in his hand."

Jaku shifted from his left foot to his right, and back again, his back to the courtroom audience. I wished I could see the expression on his face.

Fukuda went on, "Mr. Cambra testified he saw you crouched down, dragging something. Technical experts from the police department testified the concrete fragments caused by the firing of the fifth and sixth bullets into the floor lodged in Mr. Lazzarini's body, in a pattern consistent with his right hand resting on his chest. The detectives stated there was blood on Mr. Lazzarini's palm, but no injury to the fingers, and said the deceased had a perfect grip on the gun—very unusual. I could continue with innumerable additional examples, but there is yet another significant reason why I find you guilty of murder—"

Norma and I whispered "Yes!" simultaneously.

"In order to enter a legitimate plea of self-defense, you would have had to show you shot Mr. Lazzarini as a last resort, after all other measures had failed. When Mr. Lazzarini drove up, and you saw he had a gun, you should have locked yourself inside your apartment and remained inside, rather than returning to face your aggressor with a gun as you claim to have done, Mr. Cardoza. Your actions are not in accord with your plea. For this, and for the aforementioned reasons, I hereby find you guilty of murder in the first degree, Mr. Cardoza."

Fukuda pounded his gavel on the wooden bench, spoke quietly with the court clerk, set the sentencing date for October 17, and pounded the gavel again. "Court dismissed," he said.

We exited the courtroom, Norma and I complaining about the sentencing being postponed for nearly six weeks. Seven of us accepted Deputy Chief Bob's invitation to lunch. A reporter and a cameraman lugging heavy equipment stepped off the escalator. Not wanting to watch as the guards escorted Jaku to prison, we piled into the elevator.

Soon we were sipping coffee and cocktails, and eating mahi-mahi and lobster at a classy restaurant. Bob insisted lunch was his treat. "A payback," he said, and proceeded to tell us a story I'd already heard about Vic saving his life during a fuel tank fire back in '82.

I wondered if I owed my life to Vic as well. Would Jaku have killed me after he raped me? *Thanks to you, Vic, I'll never know.*

"The shame of it is, Jaku lied about what was said that morning." Bob shook his head. "So we'll never know what the argument was really about."

I know. I even know what Vic was saying. "Leave Liz alone. She's mine. I love her, I want to marry her, and you're getting in the way." *But I can't tell you or the others, Bob, not now, maybe not ever. Well, we know the truth, don't we, Vic?*

"So be it," Norma said. "I, for one, thank the good Lord that little worm will be in prison where he belongs."

Chapter 11

After the Trial

On October 17, Judge Fukuda sentenced Jaku to life in prison for first-degree murder. The judge denied Soon's motion that, because a firearm was used, Jaku should serve a minimum of fifteen years before being considered for parole. "It is the prerogative of the parole board to set the minimum sentence," Fukuda said.

The judge's ruling disappointed Norma, me, and Vic's coworkers and family, especially his sister, Betty, who flew in for the sentencing. After the guards handcuffed Jaku and led him away, seventeen of us celebrated with a lobster dinner at a restaurant overlooking a forest of sailboat masts at Honolulu Harbor.

The parole board set Jaku's minimum at ten years.

I have never seen him since.

* * *

The hullabaloo was finally over. I had been focused on the trial, and watching Jaku get put away, but now nothing distracted me from my grief. Warm, bright, breezy days seemed filled with tattered shadows stretching endlessly before me. The pain of loss rained down on me so heavily I nearly drowned. For months, I cried.

On Valentine's Day 1986, a year after Vic died, I awoke in the wee hours of the morning compelled to write about him. Grabbing a pen and paper, I wrote nonstop for two hours about things he'd done, and things we never did but might have done if only he had lived. When I lay my pen down, I felt less lonely and more connected to Vic. *This is my way to stay in touch with him.*

Weeks of sifting through memories followed. Three or four times a week, I woke up early after getting home late and scribbled down something, anything, about Vic for at least fifteen minutes before collapsing on my bed and sleeping some more. After several months of this, I realized writing through the grief was also a way for me to nurture myself so healing could begin.

Two months later, in April, I wrote a letter to Vic, which I rewrote and edited and cried over and edited some more. Finally, surrounded by Vic's shell chandelier, record albums, and hanging aquarium with bright blue beta fish swimming inside, I read the letter aloud. Then I stuffed the tear-smeared pages into a folder, to be reread on the day I finished writing Vic's book.

* * *

Seven years later, burned out on shift work, I transferred into the headquarters building on Whaler where I became a clerk, then a division secretary.

Discouraged by the clichés cluttering my writing when I tried to capture Vic's energy on paper, I wrote about Vic only sporadically. Instead, I focused on the kind of writing I easily found publishers for—non-fiction magazine articles. Writing dozens of these taught me how to organize, hook readers, write clearly and concisely, interview, and do research. My writing avocation turned into a part-time, paid vocation. Seeing my byline in several magazines gave me the encouragement I needed to continue writing.

Three years later, in April 1996, I woke up remembering a dream in which Vic urgently beckoned me to the fire station. I phoned a former coworker, Kimo, and asked him if I could drop by the next day to chat with him and the other old-timers.

"Sure, stranger," he said. "How you been the last three years since you ran out on us? Naa, naa, only joke. We'd love to see you."

On the following day, I hurried from the fire department parking lot to the shelter of the open bay garage moments before dark storm clouds blotting out the sun burst open. Inside the community room, except for a larger television fronted by leather recliners, everything looked the same. I glanced outside through rain-splattered picture windows. Beyond a nearby taxiway and distant runway, clouds camouflaged the craggy tops of the Waianae Mountains to the west.

Six of us traded small talk as gusting trade winds pelted raindrops against the station, hard, like the rapid fire from an M-16 rifle. The vets among us glanced nervously around. I felt a sharp twinge of pain, remembering how Vic died. Kimo must have been thinking about him, too, because he asked me, "Anybody tell you Vic's old bunkroom is haunted?"

"No. Really?" I shivered.

Kimo nodded, his black eyes staring. "No joke, Lizzy." He pointed to two large koa-wood-framed whale prints on the wall. "Remember the plaque used to be under those pictures? It said, 'In Memory of Victor E. Lazzarini.'"

"Of course I remember." How could I forget? I had watched and wept when a firefighter nailed the plaque to the wall below the prints donated by Vic's family eleven years previously.

"The day before last month's inspection, some fool ripped the lamp off the wall above Vic's old bunk," Kimo said. "No time to install a new lamp, so Chief said to cover the exposed wires with the plaque." He shook his head. "Ever since, the guys hear Vic yelling, 'Wake up! Wake up!' in the middle of the night. Ain't that right, Mo?"

"Damn straight." Mo ran a hand absentmindedly down the stubby length of his Mohawk haircut. "A voice jolted me awake. I thought I was dreaming, but I heard it again. I had this creepy feeling, like somebody was standing right beside me."

The guilt that had picked at me so long scratched harder.

"It happened again the next shift," Mo added. "I'm a Christian. I never believed in ghosts before. Somebody ought to bless this place."

"Somebody should," I agreed.

I soon said goodbye, retreating to my VW bug. Was I the reason Vic wasn't at peace? I had been trying to keep the promise I'd made to him after I discovered he died protecting me, to tell the truth about what happened so compellingly readers would clamor to read his story. But my words were inadequate compared to my memories of this high energy, generous, happy man. *I'll try harder, Vic. I'll hone my writing skills. I'll get you in print even if it takes me the rest of my life.*

From that day forward, I wrote at least fifteen minutes almost every day. The discovery that writing regularly nurtured me, and I sometimes gained insights just by letting my words flow onto the page, kept my fingers tapping across typewriter keys and computer keyboards. I think the skills gained from writing non-fiction articles helped me mold Vic's story into an absorbing shape. Experimenting with different forms—a screenplay, a novel (I wrote at least a dozen different versions,) and finally this memoir—also stretched my writing muscles.

Looking back, I realize my growth as a writer was another precious gift from Vic. I would not have continued writing so diligently if he hadn't dispatched me to the fire station to discover his spirit was not at peace.

As days turned into months and months turned into years, time and writing and the grace of God healed my grief. As my pain lessened, my awe increased at the memory of Vic's spirit guiding me toward the truth on that rainy day in the nursery. When his pain hit me like a cannonball, I knew I had to tell Jet my whole truth. Only then did I rediscover the dream that revealed my Prince Charming died protecting me.

December 1998 to the Present

On a windy day, two years after Kimo told me Vic's bunkroom was haunted, my heavily-muscled boyfriend, Barry, easily hoisted up Vic's weighty ceramic, teardrop-shaped, former hanging aquarium. Barry looped its braided rope onto a hook he had pounded into a wooden beam on the ceiling of our townhouse balcony.

Where two parallel, dinner-plate-shaped pieces of glass had been inset into the aquarium's sides, only one remained. A few years earlier, the weight of the aquarium, full of goldfish and water, caused the hook to straighten, the aquarium to fall, and one of the glass circles to break. My artistic sister Kay helped me pull out jagged slivers of glass, epoxy together the cracked ceramic, and rebirth the aquarium into a plant hanger.

A Mandevilla vine with cheerful yellow trumpet-like flowers bloomed inside the aquarium's cracked ceramic bowl, behind the remaining circle of glass. I wound the vine's green tendrils around the outside of the aquarium, and watched over the course of days and weeks as the vine grew flowers that bloomed and fell, growing thicker as it climbed ever higher, seeking sunlight.

Sometimes, when light from the setting sun struck the glass straight on, the aquarium shone as brightly as ten thousand candles, and seemed to pulsate with energy. At such times, I sensed Vic's spirit looking through the lens of physical life, perhaps glimpsing me sitting at my computer, writing about him.

* * *

Barry's nickname, Ashtar the Magnificent, came about because of his psychic—he called it psycho—ability. A week after he lifted up the former hanging aquarium, he told me, "This really big, cheerful guy wrestled me a couple of times in my dreams."

I said, "The big guy's got to be Vic."

Barry didn't say anything, and neither did I, because I didn't know what to say.

The following night, while the soulful sounds from Barry's acoustic guitar drifted in from the living room, I fell asleep worrying Vic would stop visiting me since I now lived with Barry. A few hours later, I woke up remembering Vic's energy surrounding me like an aware, joyful cloud, infusing me with the knowledge he was cool with "that righteous Ashtar dude" because he made me so happy.

By the time morning sunbeams sliced through the jalousie window glass in the bedroom, Barry had already left for work. As usual, he tucked a note under my computer mouse pad. This time it read, "I let Sleeping Beauty sleep. Let's talk tonight. Love, Barry."

In the evening, as we lay skin to skin, which, Barry said, was the best way for lovers to stay real when talking things over, he confided, "I might be a wee bit jealous of Vic."

My stomach knotted up. I took a deep breath. "I hear you. I'd be a whole lot jealous if your old girlfriend tackled me."

Barry laughed.

"But Vic wasn't my lover." My heart pounded against Barry's broad chest as I described my soul connection with Vic who, I speculated, was just doing his guardian angel duty and checking Barry out. "Vic's perceptive, because he sees how righteous you are. Unconditionally loving, too, because he's happy for me, that I'm happy with you."

"And me with you." Barry pressed me closer. "Thanks for sharing, eh? Okay, I get it—Vic's not a rival. I'm good with you loving your knight in armor, so no need worry, worry, worry, you silly rabbit. But will you tell him enough with the body slams already?"

I laughed.

Barry added, "I'm grateful to him and God, for giving me you."

"Gracias, mi amor. I'm so very grateful for you, too."

"You're my last Valentine, Lizzybeth."

"And you're mine, Ashytar."

I awoke the next morning counting my blessings, that at 48 years old, I had finally found a compassionate, spiritual, humorous man who found me enough; a man so secure within himself he understood and could really hear me.

* * *

These days, when sunrise flings shards of light through the jalousie window slats, I imagine Vic soaring, free as a bird, merging his light with those golden beams. I thank God for allowing me to experience a deep and transformative friendship with stalwart and courageous Vic.

And I thank Him for assigning a detective to the case who understood the spiritual nature of good and evil, right and wrong. I'm grateful to Jet for tormenting my conscience until telling the truth hurt less than the fear consuming me.

My fear of dying dissolved after Vic so vividly demonstrated the truth of God's promise that the soul survives the grave. Even now, from time to time, Vic moseys on by to remind me love is really all there is.

*　*　*

In February 2014, I pulled out the letter I wrote to Vic in 1986, one year after his death; the letter I had set aside to reread after editing the final pages of his book. As sunset focused its golden and purple beams on the aquarium's remaining piece of glass, the light illuminated the paper I held in my hands. I read the letter out loud:

> *Letter to that stylin' dude Vic Lazzarini*
> *Written on Valentine's Day 1986*
>
> *It doesn't seem like it's been four-and-a-half years since Irene introduced us, Vic, but the year since your death has felt like a decade. I trust your life in Heaven is filled with wonder and joy, and you continue to play and grow in consciousness.*
> *My mind turns to you often, especially when I write or dream about you. I think about how your standing up for me marked not only the beginning of our friendship but also the tragic end of your earthly life.*
> *Your playfulness delighted the child in me who longed to play. What drew you to me? Was it because we laughed a lot? You liked a good laugh, you with your bent sense of humor that resonated with mine. Was it because, after confiding in each other about our significant others, we discovered something more appealing in each other than we had found in them? Whatever the reason, I'm grateful you cared for me. I hope you know how deeply I still care for you.*
> *You were happier, more humorous and generous, and less wounded than any man I ever held dear. You lit up my life. How I miss you.*
> *So many things about you charmed me. Your humor; how*

you cracked me up when you strode into the alarm room with your stylin' dude walk, and teased me, and made me laugh until my sides ached. Your thoughtfulness and self-assurance; how, even after the chief embarrassed you about fraternizing with me, you waved me over in the crowded dining room, pointing at a chair beside you, and said, "Sit here, Snake."

I looked forward to coming to work when you were on shift, to talking with you about our relationships, hopes, frustrations, likes and dislikes—everything except the way we felt about each other. I felt like a rose in sunlight around you and wanted to be less morose and more positive like you. You were so very handsome, yet not the least bit stuck on yourself. You had such lovely, eclectic taste in music, and endless patience, to build up your weight lifters' physique with countless reps; to tape dozens of albums and radio shows onto 8-track tapes I still listen to.

I can't explain how something strong and sweet happened between us. Maybe it was because we started out as friends who loved to play. You had Molly and I had Billy, so we didn't come on to each other. By the time they were history, we had grown deep roots. The only thing left for us to do was blossom into love. You're the only man I knew as a pal for years before our friendship underwent a deep sea change. Every time Yogurt Teachah me hung out with Greased Lightning you, your sunshine chased my storm clouds away.

You were like the Earl of Pembroke, a brave knight and true. Jaku was like Claudius, casting treachery in his wake. Did you dismiss his stories about his crimes as the lies of a little guy just trying to act big? You never failed to stand up for the underdog, you with your kind heart.

I listened to Brian when he warned me, "Don't ever confront Jaku." I guarded my back around him, lied when necessary, gave him the attention he seemed to crave, and tried to do whatever else was necessary to save my okole.

In the end, of course, I didn't save it. You did. From the day I started working at Whaler, Jaku had sexual fantasies about me. I wonder if he heard the lies the Army fire captain spread about me being his red hot haole lover and believed them. Because I had a local boyfriend, Jaku probably told himself I liked all local guys. But I was obviously not interested in him. Worse yet, I was sweet on you.

Jaku's anger must have ignited when you told him to leave me alone, when you said you loved me and wanted to marry me, when you told him he was getting in the way of you and me. When you tried to extricate yourself from that one-sided friendship and simultaneously protect me from him, I'll bet he exploded. He's not wired to handle honesty. You knew how he dealt with people who "crossed" him. That's why you thought about taking your own gun.

But, in the end, you didn't. In the end, your innate goodness won out. You thought you could argue some sense into his lust-crazed, jealous head. You were such an open, happy man, you just couldn't fathom the depths of his deception and rage.

You showed me love always wins, Vic. Jaku thought he could get away with killing you, like he'd gotten away with so many other crimes. But he could not deceive God, or kill your soul, or bury our love. He's locked behind bars, but even if he makes parole, he'll still be imprisoned in his sick mind while you fly free like a bird. Free, like the country boy you were when you raced your motorcycle through the back roads of Pennsylvania.

When those six loud shots from Jaku's .357 Magnum sent shockwaves through the universe, the sound of a bell ringing was probably masked. But I'll bet one rang, and you earned your wings the moment Jaku shot the first bullet into you, the one that lodged in your spine, and paralyzed you, and caused your death. I'll bet that bell rang out because of the way you died, great heart; fearlessly, protecting a friend. Vic Lazzarini, my angel hero, I will always love you.

Epilogue

Believing every good book travels full circle, I wrapped this one up after consulting another spiritual counselor. In March 2014, I arranged for a phone reading from a psychic named James, reputed to be a clear channel when communicating with the spirits of loved ones. When I asked about former firefighter and forever friend Vic Lazzarini, James said he was waiting with some words for me.

"Vic thanks you for keeping his memory alive. He says being a book protagonist makes him a celebrity of sorts among the other spooks." James laughed.

My smile faded and my eyes stung with tears when James said Vic wouldn't hesitate to stand up for me all over again against that lily-livered liar Jaku. Heat flushed my cheeks when James added, "Vic says he wants you to spice up his book with a steamy dream love scene between him and you. He says, since you promised to tell the truth about all things spiritual, you should describe his and your sizzling soul connection, yeah?"

"He's right about the sizzling but it's so much bigger than that." I thought about Vic shaking me to my roots so beautifully every time his spirit moseyed on by. "Can Vic hear me?"

"Not every word, but some of them, and he senses others, and hears inflections," James said. "He experiences events holistically, in a much deeper, richer way than we do."

"I kind of understand. Well . . . maybe I can share what it was like for me when his joyful energy tingled through me, like bubbling champagne fizzing up in my cup, and I guzzled him down, and got giggly drunk on him."

James chuckled. "I'm turning red. Your pal says, 'Yes she can, and I can give her more than bubbly to dream about.'"

I laughed. "Vic's still such a tease. He already did. What could be more alluring than true love? He's the Adonis I fantasized about, the guy who saved five grand to marry me, the knight who courageously fought for me, the joy lifting me up when missing him brought me down. He's the inspiration to keep writing until I found my voice and fulfilled the promise I made to him, to make Angel Hero the very best book I could, and to get it published or die trying. I carry a blazing torch for him."

James remained silent for a few minutes. Then, with a catch in his voice, "Your friend is surprisingly eloquent for a gentleman with a firefighting background." His voice breaking, he repeated Vic's words, "Decades from now, this righteous Italian dude with a stylin' walk will offer an old lady his arm."

Warmth radiated through my body. James cleared his throat a few times. "Rarely have I encountered such a beneficent spirit. Give me a moment, please."

Seconds slipped slowly by, each one punctuated by the sound of my heart's loud pounding. James said softly, "You'll take his arm and smile at the dude who loved you more than his life."

Tears flooded my eyes and tingles exploded across my scalp as James continued, "Then he'll fly you across to the other side."

Acknowledgments

Sincere thanks to friends and family who took the time to read and offer feedback on the early awkward versions of this book, especially Mom, Aunt Mary, and my sister Kay. For their help with later renditions, I am indebted to my online writing group, especially Gary, Annie, Jerry, Sarah, Mona, and Cathy. In my Hawai'i writers group, feedback from my talented author friends Seestah, Queen Alice, Fran, and especially Shuly during the last three years has proved invaluable. Mahalo plenty to Jet for reading Angel Hero and helping me get the facts, just the facts, ma'am, right.

My deepest appreciation goes to my magnanimous and magnificent other half, Barry, for his unconditional love, understanding, and support of my need to make this book the best it could be. His helpful feedback and the endearing notes he tucked under my computer mouse kept me writing year after year after year. A decade ago, he wrote: "Flash! Bestselling authoress Lizbeth to appear soon on Oprah." Years later: "Hold on, Oprah, she's almost home." I am happily home now thanks to Barry, who is deliriously happy I have finally finished my book.

DID YOU ENJOY THIS BOOK?

Please leave me a review on Amazon!

Find out more about me at **http://www.authorlizbethhartz.com**
Find out about my publisher at **http://www.kwillbooks.com**

www.ingramcontent.com/pod-product-compliance
Lightning Source LLC
Chambersburg PA
CBHW031345040426
42444CB00005B/200